KU-034-225

The Scottish Literary Revival

an anthology of twentieth-century poetry

The Scottish Literary Revival

an anthology of twentieth-century poetry
edited by

George Bruce

STIRLING DISTRICT LIBRARY

Collier-Macmillan Limited, London
The Macmillan Company, New York

890102

821.08

BRU

Collier-Macmillan Limited
10 South Audley Street, London W1

The Macmillan Company, New York
Collier-Macmillan Canada Ltd, Toronto

All rights reserved. No part of this
book may be reproduced or utilised in
any form or by any means, electronic or
mechanical, including photocopying,
recording or by any information storage
and retrieval system, without permission
in writing from the Publisher.

Copyright © Collier-Macmillan Limited, 1968

Library of Congress Catalogue Card Number: 67-17497

First Printing 1968

Set in Monotype Baskerville 10 on 11 point
Printed in Great Britain by Morrison & Gibb Ltd
Edinburgh and London

00440 0128

Contents

vii

Acknowledgements

For permission to reprint poems in this anthology, grateful acknowledgement is made to the following:

Lucy M. M. Wintour: for 'Mercy o' Gode' by Pittendrigh MacGillivray.

Faber and Faber Ltd: for 'The Faithful Heart' and 'Mary's Song' by Marion Angus, from *Sun and Candlelight*.

Rhoda Spence: for 'The Queen's Bath-house, Holyrood' by Lewis Spence.

Sir Alexander Gray: for his poems 'The Three Kings' and 'The Deil o' Bogie'.

Rev. Dr. Andrew Young: for his poems 'The Mountain' and 'Loch Brandy'.

Helen B. Cruickshank: for her poem 'Shy Geordie'.

The Macmillan Company, New York: for 'The Watergaw' from *Sangschaw*, 'The Eemis Stane', 'Crowdieknowe' and 'Empty Vessel'; 'Poet's Pub', 'Ballad of the Crucified Rose' and excerpt from 'The Big Wheel' from *A Drunk Man Looks At The Thistle*; 'With The Herring Fishers', 'On the Ocean Floor', 'Lo! A Child is Born', 'The Two Parents', 'Reflections in a Slum' and 'The Glass of Pure Water' by Hugh MacDiarmid.

Faber and Faber Ltd, and Oxford University Press Inc.: for 'Childhood', 'The River', 'The Refugees', 'The Grove', 'The Gate', 'The Return', 'The Transfiguration', 'The Animals', 'One Foot in Eden', 'Scotland's Winter' and 'The Horses', from *Collected Poems* by Edwin Muir, Copyright © 1960 by Willa Muir.

Margaret W. J. Jeffrey: for 'When Shepherds Lace Their Boots' by William Jeffrey.

The National Library of Scotland: for 'The Gowk', 'The Tryst', 'The Proposal', 'The Hunt', 'Song', 'The Permanence of the Young Men' and 'The Children' by William Soutar.

Joseph Macleod: for excerpts from his poems 'The Ghosts of the Strath', 'The Men on the Rocks' and 'The Ambulance'.

William Montgomerie: for his poem 'Elegy'.

Albert D. Mackie: for his poem 'Molecatcher'.

The Hogarth Press Ltd: for 'The Voyage to Secrecy', 'The Thespians at Thermopylae' and 'Forgive Me, Sire' by Norman Cameron.

Robert Garioch Sutherland: for his poems 'Glisk of the Great', 'And They Were Richt', 'Whit Wad Verdi Say' and 'During a Music Festival'.

George Bruce: for his poems 'Kinnaird Head', 'Inheritance', 'The Curtain', 'The Fisherman' and 'Landscape and Figures'.

The Hogarth Press Ltd: for 'Summer Farm', 'Double Life', 'Edinburgh Courtyard in July', 'Byre', 'Icy Road', 'Responsibility' and 'Assisi' by Norman MacCaig.

Norman MacCaig: for his poem 'Leaving the Metropolitan Museum'.

Sorley Maclean: for his poems 'Knightsbridge, Libya', 'Death Valley' and 'Spring-Tide'.

Sydney Tremayne: for his poems 'Small Boy and Lighthouse' and 'Outpost in Winter'.

Douglas Young: for his poems 'Winter Pool' and 'Last Lauch'.

G. S. Fraser: for his poems 'Hometown Elegy', 'Meditation of a Patriot' and 'The Death of My Grandmother'.

R. Crombie Saunders: for his poem 'The Empty Glen'.

Ruthven Todd: for his poem 'Personal History, For My Son'.

Sydney Goodsir Smith: for his poems 'Elegy VI, What Wey Suld I' and 'Elegy XII, Orpheus' from *Under the Eildon Tree*.

George Campbell Hay: for his poems 'The Old Fisherman' and 'The Auld Hunter'.

W. S. Graham: for the excerpt from his poem 'The Night Fishing'.

Maurice Lindsay: for his poems 'On Seeing a Picture o Johann Christian Fischer in the National Gallery, Edinburgh', 'At Hans Christian Andersen's Birthplace, Odense, Denmark', 'School Prizegiving', 'Farm Widow', 'Picking Apples' and 'Aged Four'.

Tom Scott: for his poem 'Brand the Builder'.

Hamish Henderson: for his poems 'First Elegy, End of a Campaign' and 'Third Elegy, Leaving the City' from *Elegies for the dead in Cyrenaica*.

Alexander Scott: for his poems 'Haar in Princes Street', 'Continent o Venus', 'Sang Sonnet' and 'Birds in Winter'.

Edwin Morgan: for his poems 'King Billy' and 'The Death of Marilyn Monroe'.

Derick S. Thomson: for his poems 'Nuair a Thill mi Gh T'Uaigh' and 'Cruaidh?'.

George Mackay Brown: for his poems 'The Finished House', 'Wedding', 'Willag' and 'Saint Magnus in Birsay'.

The Hogarth Press Ltd: for 'Our Lady of the Waves' and 'Hamnavoe Market' by George Mackay Brown, from *The Year of the Whale*.

Ian Hamilton Finlay: for his poem 'Black Tomintoul'.

Alastair Reid: for his poem 'Growing, Flying, Happening'.

Iain Crichton Smith: for his poems 'Old Woman', 'Luss Village', 'A Note on Puritans', 'Schoolgirl on Speech-day in the Open Air', 'Two Girls Singing', 'Old Highland Lady Reading Newspaper' and 'Johnson in the Highlands'.

Stewart Conn: for his poems 'Todd' and 'Simon', from *Stoats in the Sunlight* published by Hutchinson and Co. Ltd.

Robin Fulton: for his poem 'Meeting in Early Winter'.

THE SCOTTISH LITERARY REVIVAL

It is now generally agreed that no Scottish poetry of great consequence was produced between the death of Burns in 1796 and 1922. To many this may seem of little importance. The riches of English poetry were readily available. This part of our birthright was treated at school and university, until the end of the last war, as practically the complete imaginative-literary experience due to anyone born in Britain. The most that could be hoped was that studies of the 'Scottish Chaucerians', Burns, Scott and Stevenson, would be placed in the context of the English literary tradition.

Now that the claim has been sustained by a fair weight of evidence that there is a Scottish Literary Revival, we know, as it was not known in 1922, except perhaps to Hugh MacDiarmid, what it means to speak with our own voice, for our own times, through the medium of literature. It is by this means we begin to know ourselves as we cannot without an imaginative mode of expression. The recognition has not always been pleasant.

In August 1922 the first number of *The Scottish Chapbook* was published from Montrose. Its motto printed on the front cover was 'Not Traditions—Precedents'. The Editor was C. M. Grieve. He also wrote in the magazine under the pseudonym of Hugh MacDiarmid. The first editorial carried these words: 'In my opinion, then, for several generations Scottish literature has neither seen, nor heard, nor understood what was taking place around it. For that reason it remains a dwarf among giants. Scottish writers have been terrified to appear inconstant to established conventions.... They have stood still and consequently been left behind in technique and ideation. Meanwhile the Scottish nation has been radically transformed in temperament and tendency; Scottish life has been given a drastic reorientation, with the result that Scottish literature today is in no sense representative or adequate.'

One might have thought in the light of this statement that the least promising medium for a new poetry—a poetry that would respond to a non-traditional and complex environment—was Scots. Scots had been kept alive as a literary vehicle by writers of dialect poetry, the most notable being the Aberdeenshire poet, Charles Murray, and he was one of the very few who also kept the 'mither' tongue in touch with an older and broader literary tradition by means of his translations of Horace. At the same time, some of his poems suffered from the characteristic affliction of a dying literature, a nostalgic sentimentality. This defect was, however, corrected in many poems by the density of his Scots which gave an honest sturdiness to his verses.

Had MacDiarmid's unqualified statement, '. . . the Scottish nation has been radically transformed in temperament and tendency', been wholly true, then the traditional tongue, or even variants of it, would not have been a possible basis for the poetry he was to write. There was, in fact, no recent adequate literary tradition on which he could build. As far as he was concerned the versifiers of that day were concerned with domestic irrelevancies and rhythms and forms suitable only for their own limited purposes. MacDiarmid found Murray's complete unconsciousness of the cultural plight of Scotland insufferable. But today Murray's realisation of character by means of the laconic, sardonic, Aberdeenshire idiom remains of interest; a speech that arose out of the necessities of a life made arduous and hazardous by nature. The characteristic feature of the idiom is a calculated understatement. This is a protective device against the dangers of despair or ecstasy. When the floods rose a farmer is reputed to have remarked that it was 'gey dewy'. When a man is in good health he will go no further than say he is 'nae bad'. This shrewd, humorous means of assessing life does not lead to the highest poetry but it has been the salt that has kept the savour in verse of quality that may be found in this anthology from Alexander Gray through William Soutar and Robert Garioch to Douglas Young's 'Last Laugh'. Behind the humour there is a serious attitude to life. When this seriousness is absent the humour is liable to turn to pawkiness and whimsy, two great corrupters of Scottish life and literature.

In the third issue of *The Scottish Chapbook* (October 1922) MacDiarmid stated: 'The general aim of the Chapbook is, of course, to conduct experiments into the assimilability into literature of the whole range of Scottish life—including the total content of Scottish minds.' In this issue he published 'The Watergaw', his first Scots Lyric. He provided this translation: 'One wet afternoon (or early evening) in the cold weather in July after the sheep shearing I saw that rare thing—an indistinct rainbow, with its shivering light, above the heavily-falling rain.' The translation may help us into the poem but it also reveals why English would not serve Mac-Diarmid's purpose at this stage. Why he turned to the Scottish vernacular he explained in number eight of *The Scottish Chapbook* thus: 'The vernacular is a vast storehouse of just the very peculiar

2

and subtle effects which modern European literature in general is assiduously seeking and if the next century is to see an advance in mental science equal to that which the last century has marked in material science, the resumption of the Scots vernacular in the main stream of European letters is in a fashion . . . inevitable. The vernacular is a vast unutilised mass of lapsed observation. . . . There are words and phrases in the vernacular which thrill me with a sense of having been produced as a result of mental processes entirely different from my own and much more powerful. They embody observations of a kind which the modern mind makes with increasing difficulty and weakened effect.'

MacDiarmid's early lyrics have been described as musical and graceful. This, I think, is the wrong emphasis. His own remarks about 'The Eemis Stane' show how much he is in earnest about his idea of poetry as a means of advancing the boundaries of consciousness. In these lyrics we embark on a voyage as mysterious as that journey undertaken by Thomas the Rhymer when he went to a place beyond the ends of the earth. MacDiarmid, with the knowledge that the stars are stones, looks back from space to marvel at earth's mystery. His is a mental journey concerned with the strangeness of mortal life on a small planet, which in his image is simply, yet marvellously, a stone. The celebration of life itself has remained a pre-occupation of MacDiarmid's throughout his long poetical life. The image of the moon presides in these early lyrics; later it is the sun, and later still, the image of water.

These lyrics gave no hint of the poems of social criticism that were to follow, the greatest of which is *The Drunk Man Looks at the Thistle*. The irony already mentioned as indigenous to the old tongue, was used by MacDiarmid in *The Drunk Man* to flay the Mediocrities in the Scottish social scene. The social aspects of the poem are counterpointed by variations in tone and stress that range from the comic creation of drunks in conversation at the beginning of the poem to the dream-like world of the old ballads. In this poem, for his purpose, he adapts and translates such writers as Rilke and Blok.

Thereby MacDiarmid gave a new seriousness and range to Scottish poetry. He had given it a place in the European scene. He reinstated Scots as a serious literary language. And in this achievement he had, incidentally, landed some younger writers with a problem.

MacDiarmid's synthetic Scots, as it unhappily has been called, was based on a Scots that he himself spoke, and which he heard all about him in the Borders. To this day the English he speaks is closer to Scots or Lallans than to anything spoken south of the Tweed. Hence in all his poetry in Scots the language has authority, no matter how much vocabulary he may have added by consulting literary sources for Scots words. The case of William Soutar was similar. He was brought up in a Scots-speaking home. When, however, younger writers who did not use the tongue in their youth turned to Lallans (or Scots) in admiration of MacDiarmid and deliberately thickened their Scots, the poem frequently rang false. The final test, however, is not how much bad poetry they wrote but how much good. Sydney Goodsir Smith, after a shaky start, in which he wrote romantic lyrics in Lallans, found an ironic idiom which owed something to MacDiarmid's *Drunk Man* but which bore the imprint of a fantasy that belonged to Goodsir Smith only.

In *A Drunk Man Looks at the Thistle* MacDiarmid created images of the Scots, some comical, some serious. Throughout, MacDiarmid made critical comment on Scotland. In Sydney Smith's 'Under the Eildon Tree' he laments the loss of his loves in XVI variations, but this is just the story on the surface. In the course of the poem he presents a romantic and comic view of the life about him, and in one passage a comic view of himself. He brings Mary, Queen of Scots, Knox and Stalin suddenly together. These various interests are held together by Smith's very personal comment which he makes in short throw-away lines that seem to arrive on the page as an afterthought. These lines puncture the high protestation of romantic love. In their natural modern Scots idiom we hear not only Smith's voice but the voice of people in pubs and in the streets who will not be hoodwinked by show. He has drawn on the communal life that still goes on in Edinburgh and in this poem he is the true heir to Scotland's urban poet of the eighteenth century, Robert Fergusson. He also owes a debt for the form of his poem to Ezra Pound's 'Homage to Sextus Propertius', to Pound who for many years ransacked literature from Rome to China to find styles adequate to deal with the 'modern' situation. In 'Under the Eildon Tree' Smith did in 1951 precisely what MacDiarmid had committed himself to doing in 1922. He brought Scots into touch with 'modern techniques and ideation'. But how much longer the Lallans movement can be sustained today depends on a new generation. The Scots that is spoken today is thinner than even twenty years ago and fewer people speak it, but the strength of the idiom should not be underrated. The racy, independent, life of Glasgow and the other cities goes on. There is still a treasury there.

The great problem of making a new poetry in Scots, with wide interests which were relevant to what was happening, was how to

4

develop a dying tradition. To use contemporary European poetry as part of a Scots poem was one of MacDiarmid's unexpected achievements in *A Drunk Man Looks at the Thistle*. Perhaps equally surprising and successful, though the ground had been prepared by MacDiarmid, was Sydney Smith's absorption of Pound's style into 'Under the Eildon Tree'. This was not the problem of the poets who wrote in English. Theirs was more a question of achieving an identity. More than forty years after MacDiarmid's early lyrics Norman MacCaig wrote these lines:

> Clean in the mind, a new mind creeps to being,
> Eating the old. . . . Ancestors have no place
> In such clean qualities as time and space.

So Norman MacCaig in his poem 'Aspects' had found his vantage from which he might write a poem. He writes evaluating experience without first referring to political or religious loyalties. Yet his awareness that he must hold his experience in the mind, present it and examine it with the honesty of a good scientist relates him to the Scottish philosopher, David Hume, and to the Scottish poet, John Davidson; Hume the philosopher of common sense; Davidson the poet who tried to define a snowflake with scientific accuracy in a poem. MacCaig owes nothing to either for his poetic equipment, that is to say, for the craft whereby he brings us into the image he creates or detaches us from the experience in which he has involved us. We share MacCaig's maturity when we live along with intellectual, animal-like people in the van in 'Icy Road' or when we feel horror and pity for the beggar in 'Assisi'. This is MacCaig's identity. Sharply and firmly he plants his landscapes in the mind.

George Mackay Brown, in Orkney, has a different relation with his environment. He makes his poems out of traditional Orkney but they are not simply local poems, for his Orkney is seen and felt as growing directly out of the ancient, northern Christian world. His modern Orkneymen are Vikings still challenging the sea and the land, still involved in the ceremonies of birth, marriage and death. The modern Orkney farmer with his tractor in Brown's imagination is subject to the same ultimate conditions of life and death as his forebear with the wooden plough. He is simply one of the folk.

Edwin Morgan, in Glasgow, handles folk material of a different kind but which comes to him as inevitably as George Mackay Brown's fishermen and farmers. His 'King Billy' and attendant Orangemen already belong to Glasgow mythology, even though the Protestant marchers with their anti-Pope banners still parade. Out of the mean hates that the rallies have sometimes generated, Edwin

Morgan has salvaged some humanity. In a similar way he has presented and examined the case of the cinema star, Marilyn Monroe, and found the failure of her life more in the society which failed to give her life meaning than in herself. Just as the formal structure of George Mackay Brown's poems with liturgical-like phrases and repetitions is called for by his material so Edwin Morgan's freer forms and conversational tone are appropriate to his purpose. He has looked at those people who are legends and found the suffering human being. In an urban society, and we are now considering writing in the central industrial belt of Scotland, the scaling down of the legend to human proportions and the understanding of the human plight is surely the true poetical way in this situation.

Maurice Lindsay is another poet from Glasgow who in recent years especially has made poems from his experience of people. The first person a poet must know is himself. As a poet he must come to know the tone of voice which is peculiarly his. This recognition has proved to be more difficult in Scotland than in England because we have more choices. A poet may have a Gaelic background and even if he does not write in Gaelic this will, or should, affect his expression. He may be born into a home in which no Scots is spoken and he may have been brought up to read English literature only. Maurice Lindsay's early poems are based on the English poets of the 'thirties, particularly on W. H. Auden. At that time he made his observations on people in a conversational tone and carefully controlled rhythm. Some of the poems in their evaluation of experience were surprisingly mature for a man in his early twenties. Then he discovered the rich Lallans poetry of MacDiarmid. With other young poets of the 'forties he took up the battle-cry of a poetry in dense Scots. Such successes as he scored in this vein were in short musical lyrics. Many of the words and phrases that were absorbed into the lyrics were too far divorced from Linday's own speech to be helpful in his other wider purpose of searching out character. Yet something very important happened to some Lowland Scottish writers at this time. They began to practise a style which took account of their Scottish and English literary inheritance and of their social environment. The thin Scots—I prefer this term to Lallans—Lindsay uses in his poem about Johann Christian Fischer gives a kind of period solidity to the picture. The emphasis is on firmness and discernment rather than on sentiment. Temper, not sentiment, is a distinctive characteristic of the twentieth-century Scottish poet who writes in English. The step from using a thin Scots to English is short. The English poems which Lindsay now

6

rites show the same reflective, charitable mind at work, frequently
n characters who are not viewed sympathetically today. Linday's
nguistic problems were not necessarily those of other writers.
lexander Scott came from a braid-Scots speaking environment.
Once he had adopted the Aberdeenshire tongue as a basis for his
oetry there was no question as to its authenticity. The temper in
is Scots poetry was there from the beginning.

The decisive factor in every case, no matter from where the poet
omes, is that he lives in the modern world. No matter how far he
aay be from the industrial conurbations, that destructive and disturb-
g world is with him immediately by means of the communication
y mass media. He may write in the ancient language of Gaelic but
e will still be a modern poet. We can observe, even in translation,
aat Sorley Maclean and Derick Thomson belong to the present.
a Sorley Maclean's 'Death Valley' there is the same discipline of
ind and feeling and awareness of common humanity as is in some
 the finest recent English poetry, but the phrase, even in English,

> . . . . he
> showed no pleasure in his
> death . . . . . . '

veals the origin of that discipline is in another culture. The carry
ver from that culture can be observed in the poetry of Iain
richton Smith. He ends his poem 'Money-Man' with the words,

> 'I know no crime graver than not to care.'

he quality of 'gravitas' was singularly lacking from the post-
urnsian Lowland Scots verses about burnies and bairnies in which
e, 'Scotch,' indulged our feelings too readily.

About what does Iain Crichton Smith, who was born in Lewis
ad who lives in Oban, care? His subjects are the people and places
aat are about him, people and places as they are now but carrying
 them the evidence of his and their past. In a broadcast talk Iain
richton Smith said: 'I have always believed in a poetry which
ontains fighting tensions and not in a poetry of statement.' So he
rites about people under duress as in 'Old Woman' and he allows
eas associated with theology, a subject of great concern over many
enerations to his people, to play a part in the making of his poetry.
e acknowledges this subject in the title of his latest book—*The Law
d the Grace*. But the poet's business is not simply to exhibit tensions.
he Gaelic culture and the discipline of English literature have
ven him the equipment to express and control the experiences to
hich he has laid himself open.

7

My last remark 'experience to which he laid himself open' bring us to Edwin Muir, a poet who chronologically should have been considered near the beginning of this essay, but modern Scottish poetry is polarised between MacDiarmid and Muir. MacDiarmid progressive, experimental, political, inventive, omniverous of facts and fascinated by them and yet equally delighting in fantasy; Muir full of negative capability, as Keats called the ability to await patiently on experience and to write out of this condition.

Throughout his life Edwin Muir was, in a metaphorical sense at least, a displaced person. Poverty drove his father and mother with their children from Orkney to Glasgow, where, as a boy and young man, he experienced the chaos and indifference to human need that was to become a feature of his life as his jobs took him to various countries in Europe. In these circumstances one might have expected that his impressions would not have been co-ordinated. Yet Stephen Spender noted of his meetings with him, 'On each occasion I was struck with the integrity of purpose in his work and life, which made him seem a pilgrim rather than a wanderer like myself. Indeed he had the purpose that converted a life of shifting jobs into a spiritual pilgrimage.' Of the novelist Kafka, Muir wrote, 'The image of road comes into our minds when we think of his stories; for in spite of all the confusions and contradictions in which he was involved he held that life was a way, not a chaos.' The comment casts light on Muir as well as on Kafka. If Muir's life can be read as a pilgrimage then one must beware of applying this idea to each poem. Part of his poetic practice was to accept each testing experience as it happened and to report it faithfully: hence the sadness and sometimes sense of defeat in poems written during the last war. He began from experience whether it was a dream, as it frequently was, or an actual happening, but with his increasing conviction of the reality of the spirit his poems became increasingly visionary. The risk of the visionary poet is that his poems lose their moorings with life. Edwin Muir's were saved from this for his later poems re-interpreted the experience of his life in the light of his Christian revelation.

Forty years ago the literature of the then recent past might have suggested that Scotland was populated by quaint locals. We might have been a degenerate Thrums. Perhaps the least that can be said about this anthology, which attempts to give some account of the poetry written by Scots over the past forty years, is that the poets now apply themselves to matters of general concern. As a result the mental map of Scotland has begun to be plotted.

GEORGE BRUCE

EDITOR'S NOTE

The special intention of this book is to make readily available a selection of poems that may be said to represent fairly the central character of each author's contribution to the Scottish Literary Revival of this century. This being so, I have not scrupled to quote sections from long poems where I considered no shorter complete poem showed adequately the style and interests of certain poets. For the same reason where the character of a poet could be demonstrated in a few poems I have presented a restricted selection of his work. Thus the limited selection of Robert Garioch is no reflection on the respect I accord his poetry. I much regret the omission of Burns Singer. His only poem to suit the purpose of this book was 'The Transparent Prisoner' and this was too long for inclusion.

G. B.

PITTENDRIGH MacGILLIVRAY (1856–1938)

Mercy o' Gode

I

Twa bodachs, I mind, had a threep ae day,
    Aboot man's chief end—
    Aboot man's chief end.
Whan the t'ane lookit sweet his words war sour,
Whan the tither leuch out his words gied a clour,
But whilk got the better I wasna sure—
    I wasna sure,
    An' needna say.

II

But I mind them well for a queer-like pair—
    A gangrel kind,
    A gangrel kind:
The heid o' the ane was beld as an egg,
The ither, puir man, had a timmer leg,
An' baith for the bite could dae nocht but beg
    Nocht but beg—
    Or live on air!

III

On a table-stane in the auld Kirkyaird,
    They ca' 'The Houff',
    They ca' 'The Houff',
They sat in their rags like wearyfu' craws,
An' fankl't themsel's about a 'FIRST CAUSE',
An' the job the Lord had made o' His laws,
    Made o' his laws,
    In human regaird.

bodach—an old man   threep—conversation   clour—wallop
gangrel—tramp   heid—head   beld—bald   timmer—wooden
baith—both   for the bite—to eat   fankl't—tied themselves in a knot
regaird—regard

Twa broken auld men wi' little but jaw—
    Faur better awa
    Aye—better awa;
Yawmerin' owr things that nane can tell,
The yin for a Heaven, the ither for Hell;
Wi' nae mair in tune than a crackit bell—
    A crackit bell,
    Atween the twa.

V

Dour badly he barkit in praise o' the Lord—
    'The pooer o' Gode
    An' the wull o' Gode';
But Stumpie believ't nor in Gode nor man—
Thocht life but a fecht without ony plan,
An' the best nae mair nor a flash i' the pan—
    A flash i' the pan,
    In darkness smored.

VI

Twa dune men—naither bite nor bed!—
    A sair-like thing—
    An' unco thing.
To the Houff they cam to lay their heid
An' seek a nicht's rest wi' the sleepin' deid,
Whar the stanes wudna grudge nor ony tak' heed
    Nor ony tak' heed:
    But it's ill to read.

VII

They may hae been bitter, an' dour, an' warsh,
    But wha could blame—
    Aye—wha could blame?

jaw—talk   yawmerin'—complaining   the yin—the one   dour—glum
pooer—power   fecht—fight   smored—smothered   sair-like—sore-like
unco—strange   warsh—without zest

I kent bi their look they war no' that bad
But jist ill dune bi an' driven half mad:
Whar there's nae touch o' kindness this life's owr sad
    This life's owr sad,
    An' faur owr harsh.

VIII

But as nicht drave on I had needs tak' the road,
    Fell gled o' ma dog—
    The love o' a dog:
An' tho nane wad hae me that day at the fair,
I raither't the hill for a houff than in there,
'Neth a table-stane, on a deid man's lair—
    A deid man's lair—
    Mercy o' Gode.

ill dune bi—badly done by   fell—very   gled—glad   houff—meeting place
lair—grave

MARION ANGUS (1866–1946)

The Faithful Heart

There cam' a man from Brig o' Feugh,
Whaur I was wild and young;
I kent him by his heather step
And the turn upon his tongue.

He spak' o' crofters on the hill,
The shepherd from the fauld,
Simmers wi' the flourish sweet,
Winters dour and cauld;

O' this guid man and that guid wife,
Aince lads and lassies brave,
Hoo ane still whustles at the ploo'
And ane is in his grave;

kent—knew   fauld—fold   flourish—blossom   dour—hard
ploo'—plough

O' them that's ower the faemy seas,
And them that bides at hame,
But I socht nae news o' my auld love
Nor named her bonnie name.

faemy—foamy

Mary's Song

I wad ha'e gi'en him my lips tae kiss,
Had I been his, had I been his;
Barley breid and elder wine,
Had I been his as he is mine.

The wanderin' bee it seeks the rose;
Tae the lochan's bosom the burnie goes;
The grey bird cries at evenin's fa',
'My luve, my fair one, come awa'.'

My beloved sall ha'e this he'rt tae break,
Reid, reid wine and the barley cake,
A he'rt tae break, and a mou' tae kiss,
Tho, he be nae mine, as I am his.

breid—bread   lochan—little loch   fa'—fall   mou—mouth

LEWIS SPENCE (1874–1955)

The Queen's Bath-house, Holyrood

Time that has dinged doun castels and hie toures,
And cast great crouns like tinsel in the fire,
That halds his hand for palace nor for byre,
Stands sweir at this, the oe of Venus' boures.
Not Time himself can dwall withouten floures

dinged—cast   hie—high   toures—towers   halds—holds
sweir—reluctant   oe—grandchild   boures—bowers

Though aiks maun fa' the rose sall bide entire;
So sall this diamant of a queen's desire
Outflourish all the stanes that Time devours.
Mony a strength his turret-heid sall tine
Ere this sall fa' whare a queen lay in wine,
Whose lamp was her ain lily flesh and star.
The walls of luve the mair triumphant are
Gif luve were waesome habiting that place;
Luve has maist years that has a murning face.

aiks—oaks	fa'—fall	bide—remain	sall—shall stanes—stones
tine—lose	gif—if	waesome—woeful	murning—mourning

ALEXANDER GRAY (1882–1968)

The Three Kings

There were three kings cam frae the East;
They spiered in ilka clachan:
'O, which is the wey to Bethlehem,
My bairns, sae bonnily lachin'?'

O neither young nor auld could tell;
They trailed till their feet were weary.
They followed a bonny gowden starn,
That shone in the lift say cheery.

The starn stude ower the ale-hoose byre
Whaur the stable gear was hingin'.
The owsen mooed, the bairnie grat,
The kings begoud their singin'.

spiered—asked	clachan—hamlet	lift—sky	owsen—oxen
begoud—began			

14

The Deil o' Bogie

(after the German)

When I was young, and ower young,
I wad a deid-auld wife;
But ere three days had gane by,
    Gi-Ga-Gane-by,
I rued the sturt and strife.

Sae to the Kirk-yaird furth I fared,
And to the Deil I prayed:
'O, muckle Deil o' Bogie,
    Bi-Ba-Bogie,
Come, tak the runkled jade.'

When I got hame, the soor auld bitch
Was deid, ay, deid eneugh,
I yokkit the mare to the dung-cairt,
    Ding-Dang-Dung-cairt,
And drove her furth—and leuch!

And when I cam to the place o' peace,
The grave was howked, and snod:
'Gae canny wi' the corp, lads,
    Ci-Ca-Corp, lads,
You'll wauk her up, by God!

Ram in, ram in the bonnie yird
Upon the ill-daein wife.
When she was hale and herty,
    Hi-Ha-Herty,
She plagued me o' my life.'

But when I gat me hame again,
The hoose seemed toom and wide.
For juist three days I waited,
    Wit-Wat-Waited,
Syne took a braw young bride.

wad—wed   deid-auld—dying-old   sturt—quarrel   runkled—wrinkled
soor—sour   howked—dug   snod—tidy   yird—earth
ill-daein—ill-doing   toom—empty

15

In three short days my braw young wife
Had ta'en to lounderin me.
'Gie's back, dear Deil o' Bogie,
        Bi-Ba-Bogie,
My auld calamitie!'

lounderin—beating

ANDREW YOUNG (b. 1885)

The Mountain

The burn ran blacker for the snow
And ice-floe on ice-floe
Jangled in heavy lurches
Beneath the claret-coloured birches.

Dark grouse rose becking from the ground
And deer turned sharp heads round,
The antlers on their brows
Like stunted trees with withered boughs.

I climbed to where the mountain sloped
And long wan bubbles groped
Under the ice's cover,
A bridge that groaned as I crossed over.

I reached the mist, brighter than day,
That showed a specious way
By narrow crumbling shelves,
Where rocks grew larger than themselves.

But when I saw the mountain's spire
Looming through that damp fire,
I left it still unwon
And climbed down to the setting sun.

16

Loch Brandy

All day I heard the water talk
From dripping rock to rock
And water in bright snowflakes scatter
On boulders of the black Whitewater;
But louder now than these
The silent scream of the loose tumbling screes.

Grey wave on grey stone hits
And grey moth flits
Moth after moth, but oh,
What floats into that silver glow,
What golden moth
That rises with a strange majestic sloth?

O heart, why tremble with desire
As on the water shakes that bridge of fire?
The gold moth floats away, too soon
To narrow to a hard white moon
That scarce will light the path
Stumbling to where the cold mist wreaths the strath.

HELEN B. CRUICKSHANK (b. 1886)

Shy Geordie

Up the Noran Water,
In by Inglismaddy,
Annie's got a bairnie
That hasna got a daddy.
Some say it's Tammas's
And some say it's Chay's;
An' naebody expec'it it,
Wi' Annie's quiet ways.

Up the Noran Water,
The bonnie little mannie
Is dandlit an' cuddlit close
By Inglismaddy's Annie.
Wha the bairnie's faither is
The lassie never says;
But some think it's Tammas's,
And some think it's Chay's.

Up the Noran Water,
The country folk are kind;
An' wha the bairnie's daddy is
They dinna muckle mind.
But oh! the bairn at Annie's breist,
The love in Annie's e'e!
They mak' me wish wi' a' my micht
The lucky lad was me!

muckle mind—much care   mak'—make   micht—might

HUGH MacDIARMID (b. 1892)

From *Sangschaw* (1925)

The Watergaw

Ae weet forenicht i' the yow-trummle
I saw yon antrin thing,
A watergaw wi' its chitterin' licht
Ayont the on-ding;
An' I thocht o' the last wild look ye gied
Afore ye deed!

vide: *The Scottish Chapbook* Vol. I no. 3 (p. 63) ed. Macdiarmid.
Causerie. The Rainbow. 'One wet afternoon (or early evening) in the cold weather in July after the sheep shearing I saw that rare thing—an indistinct rainbow with its shivering light above the heavily falling rain.'

Verse 1
Watergaw—rainbow   weet—wet   forenicht—evening
yow-trummle—(ewe tremble) cold spell after the sheep shearing
antrin—rare   chitterin'—shivering   licht—light   ayont—beyond
on-ding—downpour   thocht—thought   gied—gave   afore—before
deed—died

18

There was nae reek i' the laverock's hoose
That nicht—an' nane i' mine;
But I hae thocht o' that foolish licht
Ever sin' syne;
An' I think that mebbe at last I ken
What your look meant then.

Verse 2
reek—smoke   the laverock's hoose—lark's house (the sky)   nicht—night
nane—none   hae—have   sin' syne—since then

The Eemis Stane

I' the how-dumb-deid o' the cauld hairst nicht
The warl' like an eemis stane
Wags i' the lift;
An' my eerie memories fa'
Like a yowdendrift.

Like a yowdendrift so 's I couldna read
The words cut oot i' the stane
Had the fug o' fame
An' history's hazelraw
No' yirdit thaim.

Eemis stane—usually a large rock that can be rocked but does not fall
eemis—insecure   i'—in   how-dumb-deid—midnight   hairst—harvest
nicht—night   warl'—world   lift—sky   fa'—fall
yowdendrift—swirl of snow from the earth   oot—out   stane—stone
fug—moss   hazelraw—lichen   yirdit—buried   thaim—them

Crowdieknowe

Oh to be at Crowdieknowe
When the last trumpet blaws,
An' see the deid come loupin' owre
The auld grey wa's.

blaws—blows   deid—dead   loupin'—leaping   wa's—walls

Muckle men wi' tousled beards,
I grat at as a bairn
'll scramble frae the croodit clay
Wi' feck o' swearin'.

An' glower at God an' a' his gang
O' angels i' the lift
—Thae trashy bleezin' French-like folk,
Wha gar'd them shift!

Fain the weemun-folk'll seek
To mak' them haud their row
—*Fegs, God's no blate gin he stirs up*
The men o' Crowdieknowe!

grat—wept   croodit—crowded   feck—a great deal   bleezin'—blazing
gar'd—made   shift—move   weemun-folk—women
haud their row—be quiet   blate—bashful   gin—if

Empty Vessel

I met ayont the cairney
A lass wi' tousie hair
Singin' till a bairnie
That was nae langer there.

Wunds wi warlds to swing
Dinna sing sae sweet,
The licht that bends owre a' thing
Is less ta'en up wi't.

ayont—beyond   cairney—pile of stones to mark a spot   tousie—tousled
wunds—winds   dinna—do not   licht—light

From *A Drunk Man Looks at the Thistle* (1926)

Poet's Pub

(From the Russian of Alexander Blok)

At darknin' hings abune the howff
A sweet and wild and eisenin' air.
Spring's spirit wi' its waesome sough
Rules owre the drucken stramash there.

And heich abune the vennel's pokiness,
Whaur a' the white-weshed cottons lie;
The Inn's sign blinters in the mochiness,
And lood and shrill the bairnies cry.

The hauflins 'yont the burgh boonds
Gang ilka nicht, and a' the same,
Their bonnets cocked; their bluid that stounds
Is playin' at a fine auld game.

And on the lochan there, hauf-herted
Wee screams and creakin' oar-locks soon'
And in the lift, heich, hauf-averted,
The mune looks owre the yirdly roon'.

And ilka evenin', derf and serious
(Jean ettles nocht o' this, puir lass),
In liquor, raw yet still mysterious,
A'e freend's aye mirrored in my glass.

hings—hangs   abune—above   howff—inn   eisenin'—lustful
waesome—woeful   sough—willow   drucken—drunken
stramash—disturbance   heich—high   pokiness—congestion
white-weshed—white-washed   blinters—shines
mochiness—closeness (thickness of atmosphere)   lood—loud
hauflins—adolescents   'yont—beyond   boonds—bounds   gang—go
ilka—every   bluid—blood   lochan—little loch   soon'—sound
lift—sky   yirdly—earthly   roon—round   derf—bold, taciturn
ettles—intends   puir—poor   freend—friend

Ahint the sheenin' coonter gruff
Thrang barmen ding the tumblers doun
'In vino veritas' cry rough
And reid-een'd fules that in it droon.

But ilka evenin' fey and fremt
(Is it a dream nae wauk'nin' proves?)
As to a trystin'-place undreamt,
A silken leddy darkly moves.

Slow gangs she by the drunken anes,
And lanely by the winnock sits;
Frae'r robes, atour the sunken anes,
A rooky dwamin' perfume flits.

Her gleamin' silks, the taperin'
O' her ringed fingers, and her feathers
Move dimly like a dream wi'in,
While endless faith aboot them gethers.

I seek, in this captivity,
To pierce the veils that darklin' fa'
—See white clints slidin' to the sea,
And hear the horns o' Elfland blaw.

I ha'e dark secrets' turns and twists,
A sun is gi'en to me to haud,
The whisky in my bluid insists,
And spiers my benmaist history, lad.

And owre my brain the flitterin'
O' the dim feathers gangs ance mair,
And, faddomless, the dark blue glitterin'
O' twa een in the ocean there.

ahint—behind   sheenin'—shining   coonter—counter   thrang—busy
ding—throw   doun—down   reid-een'd—red-eyed   droon—drown
fey—strange   fremt—isolated (friendless)   nae—no
wauk'nin'—waking   leddy—lady   lanely—lonely   winnock—window
frae—from   atour—out over   rooky—misty   dwamin'—overpowering
wi'in—within   aboot—about   gethers—gathers   fa'—fall
clints—rocky shelves   gi'en—given   bluid—blood   spiers—asks
benmaist—innermost   owre—over   ance—once   mair—more
faddomless—fathomless   een—eyes

22

My soul stores up this wealth unspent,
The key is safe and nane's but mine.
You're richt, auld drunk impenitent,
I ken it tae—the truth's in wine!

e's—none other's   richt—right

Ballad of the Crucified Rose

I saw a rose come loupin' oot*
Frae a camsteerie plant.
O wha'd ha'e thocht yon puir stock had
Sic an inhabitant?

For centuries it ran to waste,
Wi' pin-heid flooers at times.
O'ts hidden hert o' beauty they
Were but the merest skimes.

Yet while it ran to wud and thorns,
The feckless growth was seekin'
Some airt to cheenge its life until
A' in a rose was beekin'.

'Is there nae way in which my life
Can mair to flooerin' come,
And bring its waste on shanks and jags
Doon to a minimum?

'It's hard to struggle as I maun
For scrunts o' blooms like mine,
While blossom covers ither plants
As by a knack divine.

'What hinders me unless I lack
Some needfu' discipline?
—I wis I'll bring my orra life
To beauty or I'm din!'

* The General Strike (May 1926)

in'—leaping   camsteerie—perverse, unmanageable   puir—poor
-such   pin-heid—pin-head   flooers—flowers   skimes—gleams
—would   feckless—purposeless   airt—direction   cheenge—change
in'—showing   mair—more   shanks—legs (stalks)
nts—stunted growths   orra—unworthy   or I'm din—before I'm done

Sae ran the thocht that hid ahint
The thistle's ugsome guise,
'I'll brak' the habit o' my life
A worthier to devise.'

'My nobler instincts sall nae mair
This contrair shape be gi'en.
I sall nae mair consent to live
A life no' fit to be seen.'

Sae ran the thocht that hid ahint
The thistle's ugsome guise,
Till a' at aince a rose loupt oot
—I watched it wi' surprise.

A rose loupt oot and grew, until
It was ten times the size
O' ony rose the thistle afore
Hed heistit to the skies.

And still it grew till a' the buss
Was hidden in its flame.
I never sae sae braw a floo'er
As yon thrawn stock became.

And still it grew until it seemed
The haill braid earth had turned
A reid reid rose that in the lift
Like a ball o' fire burned.

The waefu' clay was fire aince mair,
As Earth had been resumed
Into God's mind, frae which sae lang
To grugous state 'twas doomed.

Syne the rose shrivelled suddenly
As a balloon is burst;
The thistle was a ghaistly stick,
As gin it had been curst.

ugsome—ugly   brak'—break   a' at aince—all at once
heistit—hoisted   buss—bush   thrawn—stubborn   haill—whole
braid—broad   reid—red   aince—once   grugous—ugly   syne—the
ghaistly—ghostly

Was it the ancient vicious sway
Imposed itsel' again,
Or nerve owre weak for new emprise
That made the effort vain,

A coward strain in that lorn growth
That wrocht the sorry trick?
—The thistle like a rocket soared
And cam' doon like the stick.

Like grieshuckle the roses glint,
The leafs like farles hing,
As roond a hopeless sacrifice
Earth draws its barren ring.

The dream o' beauty's dernin' yet
Ahint the ugsome shape.
—Vain dream that in a pinheid here
And there can e'er escape!

The vices that defeat the dream
Are in the plant itsel',
And till they're purged its virtues maun
In pain and misery dwell.

Let Deils rejoice to see the waste,
The fond hope brocht to nocht.
The thistle in their een is as
A favourite lust they've wrocht.

The orderin' o' the thistle means
Nae richtin' o't to them.
Its loss they ca' a law, its thorns
A fule's fit diadem.

And still the idiot nails itsel'
To its ain crucifix,
While here a rose and there a rose
Jaups oot abune the pricks.

emprise—enterprise   lorn—forsaken   wrocht—wrought   grieshuckle—embers
farles—filaments of ash   hing—hung   roond—round   dernin'—hiding
maun—must   een—eyes   richtin'—righting   ca'—call
ain—own   jaups—splash

Like connoisseurs the Deils gang roond
And praise its attitude,
Till on the Cross the silly Christ
To fidge fu' fain's begood!

Like connoisseurs the Deils gang roond
Wi' ready platitude.
It's no' sae dear as vinegar,
And every bit as good!

The bitter taste is on my tongue,
I chowl my chafts, and pray
'Let God forsake me noo and no'
Staund connoisseur-like tae!' . . .

fidge—fidget   begood—begin   chowl—twist   chafts—jaws

Excerpt from

The Big Wheel

Oor universe is like an e'e
Turned in, man's benmaist hert to see,
And swamped in subjectivity.

But whether it can use its sicht
To bring what lies withoot to licht
To answer's still ayont my micht.

But when that inturned look has brocht
To licht what still in vain it's socht
Ootward maun be the bent o' thocht.

And organs may develop syne
Responsive to the need divine
O' single-minded humankin'.

The function, as it seems to me,
O' Poetry is to bring to be
At lang, lang last that unity . . .

oor—our   e'e—eye   benmaist—inmost   sicht—sight   brocht—brought

26

But wae's me on the weary wheel!
Higgledy-piggledy in't we reel,
And little it cares hoo we may feel.

Twenty-six thoosand years 't'll tak,
For it to threid the Zodiac;
—A single roond o' the wheel to mak'!

Lately it turned—I saw mysel'
In sic a company doomed to mell,
I micht ha'e been in Dante's Hell.

It shows hoo little the best o' men
E'en o' themsels at times can ken,
—I sune saw that when I gaed ben

The lesser wheel within the big
That moves as merry as a grig
Wi' mankind in its whirligig

And hasna turned a'e circle yet
Tho' as it turns we slide in it,
And needs maun tak' the place we get,

I felt it turn, and syne I saw
John Knox and Clavers in my raw,
And Mary Queen o' Scots ana',

And Rabbie Burns and Weelum Wallace,
And Carlyle lookin' unco gallus,
And Harry Lauder (to enthrall us).

And as I looked I saw them a',
A' the Scots baith big and sma',
That e'er the braith o' life did draw.

'Mercy o' Gode, I canna thole
Wi' sic an orra mob to roll.'
—*'Wheesht! It's for the guid o' your soul.'*

ae's—woe is	threid—thread	mell—mingle	Clavers—Claverhouse
aw—row	gallus—reckless	braith—breath	thole—endure
rra—common			

27

'*But what's the meanin', what's the sense?*'
—'*Men shift but by experience,*
'*Twixt Scots there is nae difference.*

'*They canna learn, sae canna move,*
But stick for aye to their auld groove
—*The only race in History who've*

'*Bidden in the same category*
Frae stert to present o' their story,
And deem their ignorance their glory.

'*The mair they differ, mair the same.*
The wheel can whummle a' but them,
—*They ca' their obstinacy "Hame",*

'*And "Puir Auld Scotland" bleat wi' pride,*
And wi' their minds made up to bide
A thorn in a' the wide world's side.

'*There ha'e been Scots wha ha'e ha'en thochts*
They're strewn through maist o' the various lots
—*Sic traitors are nae langer Scots!*'

'But in this huge ineducable
Heterogeneous hotch and rabble,
Why am I condemned to squabble?'

'*A Scottish poet maun assume*
The burden o' his people's doom,
And dee to brak' their livin' tomb.

'*Mony ha'e tried, but a' ha'e failed.*
Their sacrifice has nocht availed.
Upon the thistle they're impaled.

'*You maun choose but gin ye'd see*
Anither category ye
Maun tine your nationality.'

whummle—overturn   hame—home   bleat—bloated   **dee—die**
brak—break   ha'e—have   tine—lost

And I look at a' the random
Band the wheel leaves whaur it fand 'em.
                              'Auch, to Hell,
I'll tak' it to avizandum.' . . .

O wae's me on the weary wheel,
And fain I'd understand them!

And blessin' on the weary wheel,
Whaurever it may land them! . . .

But aince Jean kens what I've been through
The nicht, I dinna doot it,
She'll ope her airms in welcome true,
And clack nae mair aboot it. . . .

fand—found   clack—gossip

From *Stony Limits and Other Poems* (1934)

With the Herring Fishers

'I see herrin'.'—I hear the glad cry
And 'gainst the moon see ilka blue jowl
In turn as the fishermen haul on the nets
And sing: 'Come, shove in your heids and growl.'

'Soom on, bonnie herrin', soom on,' they shout,
Or 'Come in, O come in, and see me'
'Come gie the auld man something to dae.
It'll be a braw change frae the sea.'

O it's ane o' the bonniest sichts in the warld
To watch the herrin' come walkin' on board
In the wee sma' 'oors o' a simmer's mornin'
As if o' their ain accord.

heid—head   soom—swim   gie—give   dae—do   simmer—summer

For this is the way that God sees life,
The haill jing-bang o's appearin'
Up owre frae the edge o' naethingness
—It's his happy cries I'm hearin'.

'Left, right—O come in and see me,'
Reid and yellow and black and white
Toddlin' up into Heaven thegither
At peep o' day frae the endless night.

'I see herrin',' I hear his glad cry,
And 'gainst the moon see his muckle blue jowl,
As he handles buoy-tow and bush-raip
Singin': 'Come, shove in your heids and growl!'

jing-bang—mob   toddlin'—walking with small steps   muckle—big
bush-raip—bush-rope

From *Second Hymn to Lenin and Other Poems* (1935)

On the Ocean Floor

Now more and more on my concern with the lifted
                    waves of genius gaining
I am aware of the lightless depths that beneath them lie;
And as one who hears their tiny shells incessantly raining
On the ocean floor as the foraminifera die.

Lo! A Child is Born

I thought of a house where the stones seemed suddenly changed
And became instinct with hope, hope as solid as themselves,
And the atmosphere warm with that lovely heat,
The warmth of tenderness and longing souls, the smiling anxiety
That rules a home where a child is about to be born.
The walls were full of ears. All voices were lowered.
Only the mother had the right to groan or complain.
Then I thought of the whole world. Who cares for its travail

And seeks to encompass it in like lovingkindness and peace?
There is a monstrous din of the sterile who contribute nothing
To the great end in view, and the future fumbles,
A bad birth, not like the child in that gracious home
Heard in the quietness turning in its mother's womb,
A strategic mind already, seeking the best way
To present himself to life, and at last, resolved,
Springing into history quivering like a fish,
Dropping into the world like a ripe fruit in due time—
But where is the Past to which Time, smiling through her tears
At her new-born son, can turn crying: 'I love you'?

The Two Parents

I love my little son, and yet when he was ill
I could not confine myself to his bedside.
I was impatient of his squalid little needs,
His laboured breathing, and the fretful way he cried
And longed for my wide range of interests again,
Whereas his mother sank without another care
To that dread level of nothing but life itself
And stayed day and night, till he was better, there.

Women may pretend, yet they always dismiss
Everything but mere being just like this.

Reflections in a Slum

A lot of the old folk here—all that's left
Of them after a lifetime's infernal thrall
Remind me of a Bolshie the 'whites' buried alive
Up to his nose, just able to breathe, that's all.

Watch them. You'll see what I mean. When found
His eyes had lost their former gay twinkle.
Ants had eaten *that* away; but there was still
Some life in him . . . his forehead *would* wrinkle!

31

And I remember Gide telling
Of Valéry and himself:
'It was a long time ago. We were young.
We had mingled with idlers
Who formed a circle
Round a troupe of wretched mountebanks.
It was on a raised strip of pavement
In the boulevard Saint Germain,
In front of the Statue of Broca.
They were admiring a poor woman,
Thin and gaunt, in pink tights, despite the cold.
Her team-mate had tied her, trussed her up,
Skilfully from head to foot,
With a rope that went round her
I don't know how many times,
And from which, by a sort of wriggling,
She was to manage to free herself.
Sorry image of the fate of the masses!
But no one thought of the symbol.
The audience merely contemplated
In stupid bliss the patient's efforts.
She twisted, she writhed, slowly freed one arm,
Then the other, and when at last
The final cord fell from her
Valéry took me by the arm:
'Let's go now! She has ceased suffering!'

Oh, if only ceasing to suffer
They were able to become men.
Alas! how many owe their dignity,
Their claim on our sympathy,
Merely to their misfortune.
Likewise, so long as a plant has not blossomed
One can hope that its flowering will be beautiful.
What a mirage surrounds what has not yet blossomed
What a disappointment when one can no longer
Blame the abjection on the deficiency!
It is good that the voice of the indigent,
Too long stifled, should manage
To make itself heard.

But I cannot consent to listen
To nothing but that voice.

Man does not cease to interest me
When he ceases to be miserable.
Quite the contrary!
That it is important to aid him
In the beginning goes without saying,
Like a plant it is essential
To water at first,
But this is in order to get it to flower
And I *am concerned with the blossom.*

The Glass of Pure Water

Hold a glass of pure water to the eye of the sun!
It is difficult to tell the one from the other
Save by the tiny hardly visible trembling of the water.
This is the nearest analogy to the essence of human life
Which is even more difficult to see.
Dismiss anything you can see more easily;
It is not alive—it is not worth seeing.
There is a minute indescribable difference
Between one glass of water and another
With slightly different chemical constituents.
The difference between one human life and another
Is no greater; colour does not colour the water;
You cannot tell a white man's life from a black man's.
But the lives of these particular slum people
I am chiefly concerned with, like the lives of all
The world's poorest, remind me less
Of a glass of water held between my eyes and the sun
—They remind me of the feeling they had
Who saw Sacco and Vanzetti in the death cell
On the eve of their execution.
—One is talking to God.

I dreamt last night that I saw one of His angels
Making his centennial report to the Recording Angel
On the condition of human life.
Look at the ridge of skin between your thumb and forefinger.
Look at the delicate lines on it and how they change
—How many different things they can express—
As you move out or close in your forefinger and thumb.

33

And look at the changing shapes—the countless
Little gestures, little miracles of line—
Of your forefinger and thumb as you move them.
And remember how much a hand can express,
How a single slight movement of it can say more
Than millions of words—dropped hand, clenched fist,
Snapping fingers, thumb up, thumb down,
Raised in blessing, clenched in passion, begging,
Welcome, dismissal, prayer, applause,
And a million other signs, too slight, too subtle,
Too packed with meaning for words to describe,
A universal language understood by all,
And the angel's report on human life
Was the subtlest movement—just like that—and no more;
A hundred years of life on the Earth
Summed up, not a detail missed or wrongly assessed,
In that little inconceivably intricate movement.

The only communication between man and man
That says anything worth hearing
—The hidden well-water; the finger of destiny—
Moves as that water, that angel, moved.
Truth is the rarest thing and life
The gentlest, most unobtrusive movement in the world.
I cannot speak to you of the poor people of all the world
But among the people in these nearest slums I know
This infinitesimal twinkling, this delicate play
Of tiny signs that not only say more
Than all speech, but all there is to say,
All there is to say and to know and to be.
There alone I seldom find anything else,
Each in himself or herself a dramatic whole,
An 'agon' whose validity is timeless.

Our duty is to free that water, to makes these gestures,
To help humanity to shed all else,
All that stands between any life and the sun,
The quintessence of any life and the sun;
To still all sound save that talking to God;
To end all movements save movements like these.
India had that great opportunity centuries ago
And India lost it—and became a vast morass,
Where no water wins free; a monstrous jungle

34

Of useless movement; a babel
Of stupid voices, drowning the still small voice.
It is our turn now; the call is to the Celt.
This little country can overcome the whole world of wrong
As the Lacedaemonians the armies of Persia.
Cornwall—Gaeldom—must stand for the ending
Of the essential immorality of any man controlling
Any other—for the ending of all Government
Since all Government is a monopoly of violence;
For the striking of this water out of the rock of Capitalism;
For the complete emergence from the pollution and fog
With which the hellish interests of private property
In land, machinery, and credit
Have corrupted and concealed from the sun,
From the gestures of truth, from the voice of God,
Hundreds upon hundreds of millions of men,
Denied the life and liberty to which they were born
And fobbed off with a horrible travesty instead
—Self-righteous, sunk in the belief that they are human,
When not a tenth of one per cent show a single gleam
Of the life that is in them under their accretions of filth.

And until that day comes every true poet's place
Is to reject all else and be with the lowest,
The poorest—in the bottom of that deepest of wells
In which alone is truth; in which
Is truth only—truth that should shine like the sun,
With a monopoly of movement, and a sound like talking to
    God. . . .

EDWIN MUIR (1887–1959)

From *First Poems* (1925)

Childhood

Long time he lay upon the sunny hill,
    To his father's house below securely bound.
Far off the silent, changing sound was still,
    With the black islands lying thick around.

35

He saw each separate height, each vaguer hue,
  Where the massed islands rolled in mist away,
And though all ran together in his view
  He knew that unseen straits between them lay.

Often he wondered what new shores were there.
  In thought he saw the still light on the sand,
The shallow water clear in tranquil air,
  And walked through it in joy from strand to strand.

Over the sound a ship so slow would pass
  That in the black hill's gloom it seemed to lie.
The evening sound was smooth like sunken glass,
  And time seemed finished ere the ship passed by.

Grey tiny rocks slept round him where he lay,
  Moveless as they, more still as evening came,
The grasses threw straight shadows far away,
  And from the house his mother called his name.

From *The Narrow Place* (1943)

The River

The silent stream flows on and in its glass
Shows the trained terrors, the well-practised partings,
The old woman standing at the cottage gate,
Her hand upon her grandson's shoulder. He,
A bundle of clouts creased as with tribulations,
Bristling with spikes and spits and bolts of steel,
Bound in with belts, the rifle's snub-nosed horn
Peering above his shoulder, looks across
From this new world to hers and tries to find
Some ordinary words that share her sorrow.
The stream flows on
And shows a blackened field, a burning wood,
A bridge that stops half-way, a hill split open
With scraps of houses clinging to its sides,
Stones, planks and tiles and chips of glass and china
Strewn on the slope as by a wrecking wave

Among the grass and wild-flowers. Darkness falls,
The stream flows through the city. In its mirror
Great oes and capitals and flourishes,
Pillars and towers and fans and gathered sheaves
Hold harvest-home and Judgment Day of fire.
The houses stir and pluck their roofs and walls
Apart as if in play and fling their stones
Against the sky to make a common arc
And fall again. The conflagrations raise
Their mountainous precipices. Living eyes
Glaze instantly in crystal change. The stream
Runs on into the day of time and Europe,
Past the familiar walls and friendly roads,
Now thronged with dumb migrations, gods and altars
That travel towards no destination. Then
The disciplined soldiers come to conquer nothing,
March upon emptiness and do not know
Why all is dead and life has hidden itself.
The enormous winding frontier walls fall down,
Leaving anonymous stone and vacant grass.
The stream flows on into what land, what peace,
Far past the other side of the burning world?

The Refugees

A crack ran through our hearthstone long ago,
And from the fissure we watched gently grow
The tame domesticated danger,
Yet lived in comfort in our haunted rooms.
Till came the Stranger
And the great and the little dooms.

We saw the homeless waiting in the street
Year after year,
The always homeless,
Nationless and nameless,
To whose bare roof-trees never come
Peace and the house martin to make a home.
We did not fear
A wrong so dull and old,

So patiently told and patiently retold,
While we sat by the fire or in the window-seat.
Oh what these suffered in dumb animal patience,
That we now suffer,
While the world's brow grows darker and the
　　　world's hand rougher.
We bear the lot of nations,
Of times and races,
Because we watched the wrong
Last too long
With non-committal faces.
Until from Europe's sunset hill
We saw our houses falling
Wall after wall behind us.
What could blind us
To such self-evident ill
And all the sorrows from their caverns calling?

This is our punishment. We came
Here without blame, yet with blame,
Dark blame of others, but our blame also.
This stroke was bound to fall,
Though not to fall so.
A few years did not waste
The heaped up world. The central pillar fell
Moved by no living hand. The good fields sickened
By long infection. Oh this is the taste
Of evil done long since and always, quickened
No one knows how
While the red fruit hung ripe upon the bough
And fell at last and rotted where it fell.

For such things homelessness is ours
And shall be others'. Tenement roofs and towers
Will fall upon the kind and the unkind
Without election,
For deaf and blind
Is rejection bred by rejection
Breeding rejection,
And where no counsel is what will be will be.
We must shape here a new philosophy.

The Grove

There was no road at all to that high place
But through the smothering grove,
Where as we went the shadows wove
Adulterous shapes of animal hate and love,
The idol-crowded nightmare Space,
Wood beyond wood, tree behind tree,
And every tree an empty face
Gashed by the casual lightning mark
The first great Luciferian animal
Scored on leaf and bark.
This was, we knew, the heraldic ground,
And therefore now we heard our footsteps fall
With the true legendary sound,
Like secret trampling behind a wall,
As if they were saying: To be: to be.

And oh the silence, the drugged thicket dozing
Deep in its dream of fear,
The ring closing
And coming near,
The well-bred self-sufficient animals
With clean rank pelts and proud and fetid breath,
Screaming their arrogant calls,
Their moonstone eyes set straight at life and death.
Did we see or dream it? And the jungle cities—
For there were cities there and civilizations
Deep in the forest; powers and dominations
Like shapes begotten by dreaming animals,
Proud animal dreams uplifted high,
Booted and saddled on the animal's back
And staring with the arrogant animal's eye:
The golden dukes, the silver earls, and gleaming black
The curvetting knights sitting their curvetting steeds,
The sweet silk-tunicked eunuchs singing ditties,
Swaying like wandering weeds,
The scarlet cardinals,
And lions high in the air on the banner's field,
Crowns, sceptres, spears and stars and moons of blood,
And sylvan wars in bronze within the shield,
All quartered in the wide world's wood,
The smothering grove where there was place for pities.

We trod the maze like horses in a mill,
And then passed through it
As in a dream of the will.
How could it be? There was the stifling grove,
Yet here was light; what wonder led us to it?
How could the blind path go
To climb the crag and top the towering hill,
And all that splendour spread? We know
There was no road except the smothering grove.

The Gate

We sat, two children, warm against the wall
Outside the towering stronghold of our fathers
That frowned its stern security down upon us.
We could not enter there. That fortress life,
Our safe protection, was too gross and strong
For our unpractised palates. Yet our guardians
Cherished our innocence with gentle hands,
(They, who had long since lost their innocence,)
And in grave play put on a childish mask
Over their tell-tale faces, as in shame
For the rich food that plumped their lusty bodies
And made them strange as gods. We sat that day
With that great parapet behind us, safe
As every day, yet outcast, safe and outcast
As castaways thrown upon an empty shore.
Before us lay the well-worn scene, a hillock
So small and smooth and green, it seemed intended
For us alone and childhood, a still pond
That opened upon no sight a quiet eye,
A little stream that tinkled down the slope.
But suddenly all seemed old
And dull and shrunken, shut within itself
In a sullen dream. We were outside, alone.
And then behind us the huge gate swung open.

The Return

I see myself sometimes, an old old man
Who has walked so long with time as time's true servant,
That he's grown strange to me—who was once myself—
Almost as strange as time, and yet familiar
With old man's staff and legendary cloak,
For see, it is I, it is I. And I return
So altered, so adopted, to the house
Of my own life. There all the doors stand open
Perpetually, and the rooms ring with sweet voices,
And there my long life's seasons sound their changes,
Childhood and youth and manhood all together,
And welcome waits, and not a room but is
My own, beloved and longed for. And the voices,
Sweeter than any sound dreamt of or known,
Call me, recall me. I draw near at last,
An old old man, and scan the ancient walls
Rounded and softened by the compassionate years,
The old and heavy and long-leaved trees that watch
This my inheritance in friendly darkness.
And yet I cannot enter, for all within
Rises before me there, rises against me,
A sweet and terrible labyrinth of longing,
So that I turn aside and take the road
That always, early or late, runs on before.

The Transfiguration

So from the ground we felt that virtue branch
Through all our veins till we were whole, our wrists
As fresh and pure as water from a well,
Our hands made new to handle holy things,
The source of all our seeing rinsed and cleansed
Till earth and light and water entering there
Gave back to us the clear unfallen world.
We would have thrown our clothes away for lightness,
But that even they, though sour and travel stained,

Seemed, like our flesh, made of immortal substance,
And the soiled flax and wool lay light upon us
Like friendly wonders, flower and flock entwined
As in a morning field. Was it a vision?
Or did we see that day the unseeable
One glory of the everlasting world
Perpetually at work, though never seen
Since Eden locked the gate that's everywhere
And nowhere? Was the change in us alone,
And the enormous earth still left forlorn,
An exile or a prisoner? Yet the world
We saw that day made this unreal, for all
Was in its place. The painted animals
Assembled there in gentle congregations,
Or sought apart their leafy oratories,
Or walked in peace, the wild and tame together,
As if, also for them, the day had come.
The shepherds' hovels shone, for underneath
The soot we saw the stone clean at the heart
As on the starting-day. The refuse heaps
Were grained with that fine dust that made the world;
For he had said, 'To the pure all things are pure.'
And when we went into the town, he with us,
The lurkers under doorways, murderers,
With rags tied round their feet for silence, came
Out of themselves to us and were with us,
And those who hide within the labyrinth
Of their own loneliness and greatness came,
And those entangled in their own devices,
The silent and the garrulous liars, all
Stepped out of their dungeons and were free.
Reality or vision, this we have seen.
If it had lasted but another moment
It might have held for ever! But the world
Rolled back into its place, and we are here,
And all that radiant kingdom lies forlorn,
As if it had never stirred; no human voice
Is heard among its meadows, but it speaks
To itself alone, alone it flowers and shines
And blossoms for itself while time runs on.

But he will come again, it's said, though not
Unwanted and unsummoned; for all things,

Beasts of the field, and woods, and rocks, and seas,
And all mankind from end to end of the earth
Will call him with one voice. In our own time,
Some say, or at a time when time is ripe.
Then he will come, Christ the uncrucified,
Christ the discrucified, his death undone,
His agony unmade, his cross dismantled—
Glad to be so—and the tormented wood
Will cure its hurt and grow into a tree
In a green springing corner of young Eden,
And Judas damned take his long journey backward
From darkness into light and be a child
Beside his mother's knee, and the betrayal
Be quite undone and never more be done.

From *One Foot in Eden* (1956)

The Animals

They do not live in the world,
Are not in time and space.
From birth to death hurled
No word do they have, not one
To plant a foot upon,
Were never in any place.

For with names the world was called
Out of the empty air,
With names was built and walled,
Line and circle and square,
Dust and emerald;
Snatched from deceiving death
By the articulate breath.

But these have never trod
Twice the familiar track,
Never never turned back
Into the memoried day.
All is new and near
In the unchanging Here

Of the fifth great day of God,
That shall remain the same,
Never shall pass away.

On the sixth day we came.

One Foot in Eden

One foot in Eden still, I stand
And look across the other land.
The world's great day is growing late,
Yet strange these fields that we have planted
So long with crops of love and hate.
Time's handiworks by time are haunted,
And nothing now can separate
The corn and tares compactly grown.
The armorial weed in stillness bound
About the stalk; these are our own.
Evil and good stand thick around
In the fields of charity and sin
Where we shall lead our harvest in.

Yet still from Eden springs the root
As clean as on the starting day.
Time takes the foliage and the fruit
And burns the archetypal leaf
To shapes of terror and of grief
Scattered along the winter way.
But famished field and blackened tree
Bear flowers in Eden never known.
Blossoms of grief and charity
Bloom in these darkened fields alone.
What had Eden ever to say
Of hope and faith and pity and love
Until was buried all its day
And memory found its treasure trove?
Strange blessings never in Paradise
Fall from these beclouded skies.

Scotland's Winter

Now the ice lays its smooth claws on the sill,
The sun looks from the hill
Helmed in his winter casket,
And sweeps his arctic sword across the sky.
The water at the mill
Sounds more hoarse and dull.
The miller's daughter walking by
With frozen fingers soldered to her basket
Seems to be knocking
Upon a hundred leagues of floor
With her light heels, and mocking
Percy and Douglas dead,
And Bruce on his burial bed,
Where he lies white as may
With wars and leprosy,
And all the kings before
This land was kingless,
And all the singers before
This land was songless,
This land that with its dead and living waits the
    Judgment Day.
But they, the powerless dead,
Listening can hear no more
Than a hard tapping on the sounding floor
A little overhead
Of common heels that do not know
Whence they come or where they go
And are content
With their poor frozen life and shallow banishment.

The Horses

Barely a twelvemonth after
The seven days war that put the world to sleep,
Late in the evening the strange horses came.
By then we had made our covenant with silence,
But in the first few days it was so still
We listened to our breathing and were afraid.
On the second day

The radios failed; we turned the knobs; no answer.
On the third day a warship passed us, heading north,
Dead bodies piled on the deck. On the sixth day
A plane plunged over us into the sea. Thereafter
Nothing. The radios dumb;
And still they stand in corners of our kitchens,
And stand, perhaps, turned on, in a million rooms
All over the world. But now if they should speak,
If on a sudden they should speak again,
If on the stroke of noon a voice should speak,
We would not listen, we would not let it bring
That old bad world that swallowed its children quick
At one great gulp. We would not have it again.
Sometimes we think of the nations lying asleep,
Curled blindly in impenetrable sorrow,
And then the thought confounds us with its strangeness.
The tractors lie about our fields; at evening
They look like dank sea-monsters couched and waiting.
We leave them where they are and let them rust:
'They'll moulder away and be like other loam.'
We make our oxen drag our rusty ploughs,
Long laid aside. We have gone back
Far past our fathers' land.
                              And then, that evening
Late in the summer the strange horses came.
We heard a distant tapping on the road,
A deepening drumming; it stopped, went on again
And at the corner changed to hollow thunder.
We saw the heads
Like a wild wave charging and were afraid.
We had sold our horses in our fathers' time
To buy new tractors. Now they were strange to us
As fabulous steeds set on an ancient shield
Or illustrations in a book of knights.
We did not dare go near them. Yet they waited,
Stubborn and shy, as if they had been sent
By an old command to find our whereabouts
And that long-lost archaic companionship.
In the first moment we had never a thought
That they were creatures to be owned and used.
Among them were some half-a-dozen colts
Dropped in some wilderness of the broken world,
Yet new as if they had come from their own Eden.

46

Since then they have pulled our ploughs and borne our loads,
But that free servitude still can pierce our hearts.
Our life is changed; their coming our beginning.

WILLIAM JEFFREY (1896–1946)

When Shepherds Lace Their Boots

When shepherds lace their boots at dawn
   And dogs stretch for the hill,
The lark within his globe of song
   Thinks all things mark his skill.

But through the dark and stubborn clay
   A worm churns in its slime
And sees not wing by quivering wing
   Uphold the living chime.

For him, since Adam spat on hand,
   The first spade trenched the soil,
Lark-song and soar have been a vain
   Expenditure of toil.

WILLIAM SOUTAR (1898–1943)

The Gowk

Half doun the hill, whaur fa's the linn
Far frae the flaught o' fowk,
I saw upon a lanely whin
A lanely singin' gowk:
Cuckoo, cuckoo;
And at my back
The howie hill stüde up and spak:
Cuckoo, cuckoo.

gowk—cuckoo   fa's—falls   flaught—bustle   fowk—folk
lanely—lonely   whin—gorse-bush   howie—hollow

There was nae soun': the loupin' linn
Hung frostit in its fa':
Nae bird was on the lanely whin
Sae white wi' fleurs o' snaw:
Cuckoo, cuckoo;
I stüde stane still;
And saftly spak the howie hill:
Cuckoo, cuckoo.

soun'—sound   loupin'—leaping   fleurs—flowers   saftly—softly

The Tryst

O luely, luely cam she in
And luely she lay doun:
I kent her be her caller lips
And her breists sae sma' and roun'.

A' thru the nicht we spak nae word
Nor sinder'd bane frae bane:
A' thru the nicht I heard her hert
Gang soundin' wi' my ain.

It was about the waukrife hour
Whan cocks begin to craw
That she smool'd saftly thru the mirk
Afore the day wud daw.

Sae luely, luely, cam she in
Sae luely was she gaen
And wi' her a' my simmer days
Like they had never been.

luely—softly   be—by   caller—fresh   sinder'd—sundered
bane—bone   gang—go   ain—own   waukrife—wakeful
smool'd—slipped away   mirk—darkness   daw—dawn
simmer—summer

The Proposal

(A Whigmaleerie)

Rab Kelty was a widow-man;
But that was nocht byor'nar,
Sin three guid-wives were doun at Dron
A' kistit in ae corner.

As comfort for the hindmaist ane
He courtit Minnie Summers;
And ae day brocht her to the stane
That was abüne his kimmers.

Rab look't a whilie at the lair
Syne wi a sech said: 'Hinny,
Hoo wud ye like to be happit here?'
'I wudna mind,' said Minnie.

nocht—nothing   byor'nar—extraordinary   kistit—coffined
hindmaist—most recent   kimmers—gossips   whilie—a little while
lair—burial ground   syne—then   hinny—honey   happit—buried

The Hunt

(From a German Folk-song)

I stüde upon a green holt,
Abüne a windy muir,
Whan the sma', white rose was fa'in
Doun through the simmer air.

Sae saftly cam the wind's sound;
Sae saftly dee'd awa:
And aye the gowk wud sing *cuckoo*
Frae the schedow o' the schaw.

abüne—above   muir—moor   sma'—small   fa'in—falling
simmer—summer   saftly—softly   dee'd—died   gowk—cuckoo
schedow—shadow   schaw—grove

49

But like a clap o' thunder
That whudders in a crack,
The hunter's horn rang owre the muir
And the hill gien it back.

The hunter rade a bluid-reid horse
And blew a siller horn;
And weel I kent as he gaed by
He socht the unicorn.

But the unicorn is rauchlie
And comes o' gentle birth;
And kens that God has wal'd him oot
Abüne a' baes on earth.

The unicorn is rauchlie
And rins upon the hicht;
Nor fastest fit can forret him
Nor hand can mank his micht.

Up gaed the frawfu' hunter;
Sae saft I heard him blaw;
And saftly cam *cuckoo, cuckoo*
Frae the schedow o' the schaw.

I stüde upon a green holt,
Abüne a windy muir,
Whaur the sma', white rose was fa'in
Doun through the simmer air.

whudders—makes a rushing sound   bluid-red—blood-red   siller—silver
weel—well   socht—sought   rauchlie—fearless   wal'd—chosen
oot—out   baes—beasts   rins—runs   hicht—height   fit—foot
forret—forward   mank—impair   micht—might   gaed—went
frawfu'—bold

Song

Whaur yon broken brig hings owre;
Whaur yon water maks nae soun';
Babylon blaws by in stour:
Gang doun wi' a sang, gang doun.

whaur—where   brig—bridge   hings—hangs   owre—over
maks—makes   nae—no   soun'—sound   blaws—blows   stour—dust

Deep, owre deep, for onie drouth:
Wan eneuch an ye wud droun:
Saut, or seelfu', for the mouth;
Gang doun wi' a sang, gang doun.

Babylon blaws by in stour
Whaur yon water maks nae soun':
Darkness is your only door;
Gang doun wi' a sang, gang doun.

onie—any   drouth—drought   wan—black   eneuch—enough
droun—drown   saut—salt   seelfu'—pleasant

The Permanence of the Young Men

No man outlives the grief of war
Though he outlive its wreck:
Upon the memory a scar
Through all his years will ache.

Hopes will revive when horrors cease;
And dreaming dread be stilled;
But there shall dwell within his peace
A sadness unannulled.

Upon his world shall hang a sign
Which summer cannot hide:
The permanence of the young men
Who are not by his side.

The Children

Upon the street they lie
Beside the broken stone:
The blood of children stares from the broken stone.

Death came out of the sky
In the bright afternoon:
Darkness slanted over the bright afternoon.

51

Again the sky is clear
But upon earth a stain:
The earth is darkened with a darkening stain:

A wound which everywhere
Corrupts the hearts of men:
The blood of children corrupts the hearts of men.

Silence is in the air:
The stars move to their places:
Silent and serene the stars move to their places:

But from earth the children stare
With blind and fearful faces:
And our charity is in the children's faces.

JOSEPH MACLEOD—'ADAM DRINAN' (b. 1903)

From

The Ghosts of the Strath

Three ghosts of old communicants
sitting at the table of the manse:
            with no people, a minister;
            with no pupils, a dominie;
and Muckle Donuil the minister's man.

Three ghosts of three old griefs
shuffling through the fallen evening:
Three ghosts of three old comrades
swallowing their doubts of Providence:

These alone came strange to the strath.
These alone remained in the strath:
            the minister and
            the dominie and
Muckle Donuil the minister's man.

From

The Men on the Rocks

Our pastures are bitten and bare
our wool is blown to the winds
our mouths are stopped and dumb
our oatfields weak and thin.
Nobody fishes the loch
nobody stalks the deer.
Let us go down to the sea.
The friendly sea likes to be visited.

Our fathers sleep in the cemetery
their boats, cracked, by their side.
The sea turns round in his sleep
pleasurecraft nod on the tide.
Sea ducks slumber on waves
Sea eagles have flown away.
Let us put out to sea.
The fat sea likes to be visited.

Fat sea, what's on your shelf?
all the grey night we wrestled.
To muscle, to skill, to petrol,
Hook oo rin yo! . . . one herring!
and of that only the head.
Dogfishes had the rest,
A parting gift from the sea.
The merry waves like to be visited.

Merry sea, what have you sent us?
A rusty English trawler?
The crew put into the hotel
the engineer overhauls her.
Gulls snatch offal to leeward.
We on the jetty await
gifts of the cod we can't afford . . .
The free sea likes to be visited.

Free were our father's boats
whose guts were strown on the shore.

Steam ships were bought by the rich
cheap from the last war.
They tear our nets to pieces
and the sea gives them our fishes.
Even he favours the rich.
The false sea likes to be visited.

The Ambulance

Now that you cannot walk
now that you cannot stand
afraid to talk
in case you cannot speak,
they have taken away on a stretcher
the thinned limbs I have loved:
like maggotty meat on a place
the brain I have worshipped.

'Zachai' in the ambulance
'Have you zachai for the bearers?'

Now that the sun is stopping
now that the paralysed moon
is gnawn away, and the stars' hands
fail at the signing of names,
they have taken away on a stretcher
not the universe itself,
but only the dying body
of the god that made it work.

WILLIAM MONTGOMERIE (b. 1904)

Elegy

(for William Soutar)

A narrowing of knowledge to one window to a door
Swinging inward on a man in a windless room
On a man inwardly singing
                    on a singing child

Alone and never alone a lonely child
Singing
         in a mirror dancing to a dancing child
Memory sang and words in a mimic dance
Old words were young and a child sang.

A narrowing of knowledge to one room to a doorway
To a door in a wall swinging bringing him friends
A narrowing knowledge to
                 an arrow in bone in the marrow
An arrow
      death
           strung on the string of the spine

To the live crystal in the palm and the five fingers
To the slow thirty years' pearl in the hand
Shelled in a skull in the live face of a statue
Sea-flowered on the neck of broken marble
Sunken fourteen years in that aquarium.

ALBERT D. MACKIE (b. 1904)

Molecatcher

Strampin' the bent, like the Angel o' Daith,
    The mowdie-man staves by;
Alang his pad the mowdie-worps
    Like sma' Assyrians lie.

And where the Angel o' Daith has been,
    Yirked oot o' their yirdy hames,
Lie Sennacherib's blasted hosts
    Wi' guts dung oot o' wames.

Sma' black tramorts wi' gruntles grey,
    Sma' weak weemin's han's,
Sma' bead-een that wid touch ilk hert
    Binnae the mowdie-man's.

strampin'—tramping vigorously   bent—grassland
mowdie-man—mole-catcher   staves—walks   mowdie-worps—moles
sma'—small   yirked—jerked   yirdy—earthy   dung—dug
wames—stomachs   tramorts—corpses   gruntles—snouts
weemin—women   bead-een—beady eyes   wid—would   ilk—every
binnae—but not

NORMAN CAMERON (1905–1953)

The Voyage to Secrecy

The morn of his departure, men could say
'Either by such a way or such a way,'
And, a week later, still, by plotting out
The course of all the roadways round about,
'In these some score of places he may be,'
How many days the voyage to secrecy?
Always the milestones by the road hark back

To whence he came, and those in idleness
Can bound his range with map and compasses.

When shall their compasses strain wide and crack,
And alien milestones, with strange figures,
Baffle the sagest of geographers?

The Thespians at Thermopylae

The honours that the people give always
Pass to those use-besotted gentlemen
Whose numskull courage is a kind of fear,
A fear of thought and of the oafish mothers
('Or with your shield or on it') in their rear.
Spartans cannot retreat. Why, then, their praise
For going forward should be less than others'.
But we, actors and critics of one play,
Of sober-witted judgment, who could see
So many roads, and chose the Spartan way,
What has the popular report to say
Of us, the Thespians at Thermopylae?

Forgive Me, Sire

Forgive me, Sire, for cheating your intent,
That I, who should command a regiment,
Do amble amiably here, O God,
One of the neat ones in your awkward squad.

ROBERT GARIOCH (b. 1909)

Glisk of the Great

I saw him comin out the N.B. Grill,
creashy and winey, wi his famous voice
crackan som comic bawr to please three choice
notorious baillies, lauchan fit to kill.

Syne thae fowre crousie cronies clam intill
a muckle big municipal Rolls-Royce,
and disappeared, aye lauchan, wi a noise
that droont the traffic, towards the Calton Hill.

As they rade by, it seemed the sun was shinan
brichter nor usual roun thae cantie three
that wi thon weill-kent Heid-yin had been dinan.

Nou that's the kinna thing I like to see;
tho ye and I look on and canna jyne in,
it gies our toun some tone, ye'll aa agree.

glisk—glimpse   N.B.—North British Hotel   creashy—greasy
bawr—bawdy joke   lauchan—laughing   fowre—four
crousie—cheerful   cronies—friends   clam—climbed   intill—into
droont—drowned   cantie—happy   thon—that   weill-kent—well-known
Heid-yin—head-one   kinna—kind of   jyne—join   gies—gives
toun—town   aa—all

And They Were Richt

I went to see 'Ane Tryall of Heretiks'
by Fionn MacColla, treatit as a play;
a wycelike wark, but what I want to say
is mair taen-up wi halie politics

nor wi the piece itsel; the kinna tricks
the unco-guid get up til when they hae
their wey. Yon late-nicht ploy on Setturday
was thrang wi Protestants and Catholics.

wycelike—wise-like   taen-up—taken up   halie—holy   kinna—kind of
til—to   hae—have   wey—way   ploy—employment   thrang—busy

58

an eydent audience, wi fowth of bricht
arguments wad hae kept them gaun till Monday.
It seemed discussion wad last out the nicht,

hadna the poliss, sent by Mrs. Grundy
pitten us out at twalve. And they were richt!
Wha daur debait religion on a Sunday?

eydent—diligent   fowth—plenty   bricht—bright   gaun—going
poliss—police   pitten—put   twalve—twelve   daur—dare

Whit Wad Verdi Say

I'm a librettist, I wad hae ye ken,
the opera's wordman, nae less, its hub;
I'd jist met my composer in a pub,
the place was thrang, jist gettan-on for ten.

What happened neist? We were twa skeelie men,
a spunk and spunk-box, wi ae orra rub,
tane on tither, fuff! the wudden stub
brenns in a lowe, the Muse does it again!

I singit owre his tune for Peggy's sang
but, stertan in the minor, wasna faur
throu the first baurs, he tellt me it was wrang,

it's in the major. Thon's a tune sall garr
the warld clap their haunds to hear, or lang.
The baurman bawled: Nae singin in the baur!

wad—would   ken—know   thrang—busy   neist—next
skeelie—skilful   spunk—match   ae—one   orra—odd
tane on tither—the one on the other   brenns—burns   lowe—glow
stertan—starting   wasna—was not   baurs—bars   thon's—that's
garr—make   warld—world   or lang—before long

During a Music Festival

Cantie in seaside simmer on the dunes,
I fling awa my dowp of cigarette
whaur bairns hae biggit castles out of sand
and watch the reik rise frae the parapet.

Suddenlike I am back in Libya;
yon's the escarpment, and a bleizan plane,
the wee white speck that feeds the lyft wi reik,
dirkins a horror-pictur on my brain.

And aye the reik bleeds frae the warld's rim
as it has duin frae Babylon and Troy,
London, Bonn, Edinbro, time eftir time.
And great Beethoven sang a Hymn to Joy.

cantie—content   simmer—summer   dowp—fag-end   biggit—built
reik—smoke   bleizan—blazing   lyft—sky   dirkins—darkens
frae—from   duin—done

GEORGE BRUCE (b. 1909)

Kinnaird Head

I go North to cold, to home, to Kinnaird,
Fit monument for our time.

This is the outermost edge of Buchan.
Inland the sea birds range,
The tree's leaf has salt upon it,
The tree turns to the low stone wall
And here a promontory rises towards Norway,
Irregular to the top of thin grey grass
Where the spindrift in storm lays its beads.
The water plugs in the cliff sides,
The gull cries from the clouds.
This is the consummation of the plain.

O impregnable and very ancient rock,
Rejecting the violence of water,
Ignoring its accumulations and strategy,
You yield to history nothing.

Inheritance

This which I write now
Was written years ago
Before my birth
In the features of my father.

It was stamped
In the rock formations
West of my hometown.
Not I write,

But, perhaps, William Bruce,
Cooper,
Perhaps here his hand
Well articled in his trade.

Then though my words
Hit out
An ebullition from
City or flower,

There not my faith,
These the paint
Smeared upon
The inarticulate,

The salt-crusted sea-boot,
The red-eyed mackerel,
The plate shining with herring,
And many men,

Seamen and craftsmen and curers,
And behind them
The protest of hundreds of years,
The sea obstinate against the land.

The Curtain

Half way up the stairs
Is the tall curtain.
We noticed it there
After the unfinished tale.

My father came home,
His clothes sea-wet,
His breath cold.
He said a boat had gone.

He held a lantern.
The mist moved in,
Rested on the stone step
And hung above the floor.

I remembered
The blue glint
Of the herring scales
Fixed in the mat

And also a foolish crab
That held his own pincers fast.
We called him
Old Iron-clad.

I smelt again
The kippers cooked in oak ash.
That helped me to forget
The tall curtain.

The Fisherman

As he comes from one of those small houses
Set within the curve of the low cliff
For a moment he pauses
Foot on step at the low lintel
Before fronting wind and sun.
He carries out from within something of the dark
Concealed by heavy curtain,
Or held within the ship under hatches.

Yet with what assurance
The compact body moves,
Head pressed to wind,
His being at an angle
As to anticipate the lurch of earth.

Who is he to contain night
And still walk stubborn
Holding the ground with light feet
And with a careless gait?
Perhaps a cataract of light floods,
Perhaps the apostolic flame.
Whatever it may be
The road takes him from us,
Now the pier is his, now the tide.

Landscape and Figures

I

Whinbush, wind-beaten, flares summer.
One statement of colour only against
Rain-leaden sky, in lea of a low dyke
In rock land and salt pasture
To the round of sea. Nothing more.
No grace here, nor riches, but authority.
Here the single lark sings in the brain
(Curtailment of life by the astringent salt),
The weasel in the wall gestures at the raging
Hare making fast for, its only month, March.
Frozen in Time they utter a way
No less than Van Gogh's chair,
Shabby with pipe and ash upon it,
And no more.
            Here is authority.

II

Present now an island with multitude,
A hundred songs at once bursting the air
With larks, tumbling pee-wits till moonrise

Where orchis lights pink, blood-red and purple
The black moors rimmed by the imponderable sea,
In this theatre the ruined arch, the stone
Steps worn by the pious and the impious
To the altar and the kitchen. Oysters
And golden amontillado for the abbot,
Brown beer for the other orders.
Between the rose-garden and the rhubarb patch
The runnel grosses the kitchen fats
And through the slits in the containing wall
Out of the castle on the hill, the bulk
Of life, the visiting soldiery come
(From time to time engendering the village)
To accept the benedictions of the cross.

Proliferation, cruelty, processionals,
Motley and some grace.

III

All gone to rack-ruin: what with
Invasion, reformation, deformation,
Mildew, neglect, mould, persistence
Of air, water, heat, cold, damp,
Mere absence of persons until
The Ministry of Works clocked in
(St. Aidan, St. Cuthbert looked from
The priory to the herring sea).
'Two bob a time,' said the guide,
'Climb the wall, that's what the bastards
Do. Set foot on hallowed ground—
That's their carry on, 'less I nip round.'
Two crows sit on the arch that branched
And broke the thin blue sky.
'Two crows! That's 'em back
That stole St. Cuthbert's new straw thatch,'
The guard from the castle bawls;
'Not Sundays, Thursday's opening day,
Pubs open Sunday—all day, all day.'
Shuttered from the sun the soldiers
Push their dominoes on marble tops.
The coaches roar upon the beach.
The girls go gay in dolly hats, ribald

The toy trumpets shriek, a feast
For Bob, Tom, John. Lit up
They swelter in the westering sun.
Tonight the red-gold horses call
With klaxon music from the stalls.
A few spill over on the abbey grass,
Tom Jenkins having one too many,
Early this mild September dark
Sets in. Soundless the sea encroaches,
Salt encrusts the lovers and the rose.
Forgotten on the sand two children play,
They build an abbey with a future
That crumbles at the touch of tide.

NORMAN MacCAIG (b. 1910)

Summer Farm

Straws like tame lightnings lie about the grass
And hang zigzag on hedges. Green as glass
The water in the horse-trough shines.
Nine ducks go wobbling by in two straight lines.

A hen stares at nothing with one eye,
Then picks it up. Out of an empty sky
A swallow falls and, flickering through
The barn, dives up again into the dizzy blue.

I lie, not thinking, in the cool, soft grass,
Afraid of where a thought might take me—as
This grasshopper with plated face
Unfolds his legs and finds himself in space.

Self under self, a pile of selves I stand
Threaded on time, and with metaphysic hand
Lift the farm like a lid and see
Farm within farm, and in the centre, me.

Double Life

This wind from Fife has cruel fingers, scooping
The heat from streets with salty finger-tips
Crusted with frost; and all Midlothian,
Stubborn against what heeled the sides of ships
Off from the Isle of May, stiffens its drooping
Branches to the south. Each man
And woman put their winter masks on, set
In a stony flinch, and only children can
Light with a scream an autumn fire that says
With the quick crackle of its smoky blaze,
'Summer's to burn and it's October yet.'

My Water of Leith runs through a double city;
My city is threaded by a complex stream.
A matter for regret. If these cold stones
Could be stones only, and this watery gleam
Within the chasms of tenements and the pretty
Boskage of Dean could echo the groans
Of cart-wheeled bridges with only water's voice,
October would be just October. The bones
Of rattling winter would still lie underground,
Summer be less than ghost, I be unbound
From all the choking folderols of choice.

A loss of miracles—or an exchange
Of one sort for another. When the trams
Lower themselves like bugs on a branch down
The elbow of the Mound, they'd point the diagrams
Buckled between the New Town and the range
Of the craggy Old: that's all. A noun
Would so usurp all grammar no doing word
Could rob his money-bags or clap a crown
On his turned head, and all at least would be
Existence without category—free
From demonstration except as hill or bird.

And then no double-going stream would sing
Counties and books in the symbolic air,
Trundling my forty years to the Port of Leith.
But now, look around, my history's everywhere
And I'm my own environment. I cling

Like a cold limpet underneath
Each sinking stone and am the changing sea.
I die each dying minute and bequeath
Myself to all Octobers and to this
Damned flinty wind that with a scraping kiss
Howls that I'm winter, coming home to me.

Edinburgh Courtyard in July

Hot light is smeared as thick as paint
On these ramshackle tenements. Stones smell
   Of dust. Their hoisting into quaint
Crowsteps, corbels, carved with fool and saint,
Holds fathoms of heat, like water in a well.

   Cliff-dwellers have poked out from their
High cave-mouths brilliant rags on drying-lines;
   They hang still, dazzling in the glare,
And lead the eye up, ledge by ledge, to where
A chimney's tilted helmet winks and shines.

   And water from a broken drain
Splashes a glassy hand out in the air
   That breaks in an unbraiding rain
And falls still fraying, to become a stain
That spreads by footsteps, ghosting everywhere.

Byre

The thatched roof rings like heaven where mice
Squeak small hosannahs all night long,
Scratching its golden pavements, skirting
The gutter's crystal river-song.

Wild kittens in the world below
Glare with one flaming eye through cracks,
Spurt in the straw, are tawny brooches
Splayed on the chests of drunken sacks.

The dimness becomes darkness as
Vast presences come mincing in,
Swagbellied Aphrodites, swinging
A silver slaver from each chin.

And all is milky, secret, female.
Angels are hushed and plain straws shine.
And kittens miaow in circles, stalking
With tail and hindleg one straight line.

Icy Road

The world skates by on whatever is its icerink,
Paying out a chain in lamplight of long waltzes.
We crouch in our tiny van,
Four intellectual cavemen and a woman.

A fire of dung, one feels, should be our centre,
With fishbones here and there, and on the cave wall
Bourgeois fluently hunting
Startled ideas through a wood of cant.

Chins jolt on knees. We brush the floor with knuckles
Or clutch at the ribbed roof with a simian gesture
And bandy to and fro
Our beetlebrowed ideas, all for show.

A show to hide the show outside, the newsreel
Flickering past, projected on the darkness,
That any moment will
Come to a stop with us its stars: a still.

Responsibility

They left the horse standing for two days
With a shattered leg
Till the vet signed a paper.
Then they dug a hole beside it
And put a bullet in its skull.
They didn't consider its wishes
When they did either of those things.

This could have been worse only
If they had to wait
Till the horse signed a paper.

Some day they'll dig a hole
Near enough to the vet's bed
For him to know it's there.
Let him write that off,
Let him sign himself out of that
When he's lying there with a face on him
As white as bone.

Assisi

The dwarf with his hands on backwards
Sat, slumped, like a half-filled sack
On tiny twisted legs from which
Sawdust might run,
Outside the three tiers of churches built
In honour of St. Francis, brother
Of the poor, talker with birds, over whom
He had the advantage
Of not being dead yet.

His look owed its slyness
To the fact
That he had no neck.

A priest explained
How clever it was of Giotto
To make his frescoes tell stories
That would reveal to the illiterate the goodness
Of God and the suffering
Of His Son. I understood
The explanation and
The cleverness.

A hen-rush of tourists, clucking contentedly,
Fluttered after him as he scattered
The grain of the Word.
It was they who had passed
The ruined temple outside, whose eyes
Wept pus, whose back was higher
Than his head, whose lopsided mouth
Said *Grazie* in a voice as sweet
As a child's when she speaks to her mother
Or a bird's when it spoke
To St. Francis.

Leaving the Metropolitan Museum

I went out from the unsheltered world of art
Into the unsheltered world,
And there, by the door—
Picasso's Goat—

A shape of iron entered into by herds,
By every aspect of goatishness.—
(What are you to say of a man
Who can carve a smell, who
Can make a goat-smell out of iron?)

This is the lie of art
Telling its great truth:
A shape of iron, destructible and
Created, being a revelation about life,
That is destructive and
Indestructible.

From now on, whatever of life
Passes my understanding, I know more of it
Than I did, being
A professor of goats, a pedant
Of goatishness.

70

Knightsbridge, Libia
(an Òg mhios 1942)

Ged tha mi 'n diugh ri uchd a' bhatail
Chan ann an seo mo shac 's mo dhiachainn:
Cha ghunnachan 's cha thancan Roimeil,
Ach mo ghaol bhith coirbte briagach.

Knightsbridge, Libya
(June 1942)

Though I am today against the breast of battle,
not here my burden and extremity:
not Rommel's guns and tanks,
but that my darling is depraved and a liar.

Glaic a' Bhàis

Thuirt Nàsach air choireigin gun tug am Furair air ais do fhir na fearmailte 'a' chòir agus an sonas bàs fhaotainn anns an àraich'.)

'Na shuidhe marbh an 'Glaic a' Bhàis'
Fo Dhruim Ruidhìseit,
Gille òg 's a logan sios m' a ghruaidh
'S a thuar grìsionn.

Smaoinich mi air a' chòir 's an àgh
A fhuair e bho fhurair
Bhith tuiteam ann an raon an àir
Gun éirigh tuilleadh;

Air a' ghreadhnachas 's air a' chliù
Nach d' fhair e 'na aonar
Ged b' esan bu bhrònaiche snuadh
Ann an glaic air laomadh

71

Le cuileagan mu chlosaich ghlas'
Air gainmhich lachdainn
'S i salach-bhuidhe 's làn de raip
'S de sprùidhlich catha.

An robh an gille air an dream
A mhàb na h-Iùdhaich
'S na Comunnaich, no air an dream
Bu mhotha dhiubhsan

A threòraicheadh bho thoiseach àl,
Gun deòin, gu buaireadh
Agus bruaillean cuthaich gach blàir
Air sgàth uachdaran?

Ge b'e a dheòin-san no a chàs,
A neoichiontas no mhìorun,
Cha do nochd e toileachadh 'na bhàs
Fo Dhruim Ruidhìseit.

Death Valley

(Some Nazi or other said that the Führer had restored to German
manhood the 'right and joy of dying in battle'.)

Sitting dead in 'Death Valley'
below the Ruweisat Ridge,
a boy with his forelock down about his cheek
and his face slate-grey.

I thought of the right and the joy
he had from his Führer,
of falling in the field of slaughter
to rise no more;

of the pomp and the fame
that he had, not alone,
though he was the most piteous to see
in a valley gone to seed

72

with flies about grey corpses
on a dun sand,
dirty-yellow and full of the rubbish
and fragments of battle.

Was the boy of the band
who abused the Jews
and Communists, or of the bigger
band of those

led from the beginning of generations,
unwillingly, to the trials
and mad delirium of every war
for the sake of rulers?

Whatever his desire or mishap,
his innocence or malignity,
he showed no pleasure in his death
below the Ruweisat Ridge.

Reothairt

Uair is uair agus mi briste
Thig mo smuain ort is tu òg
Is lìonaidh an cuan do-thuigsinn
Le làn-mara 's mìle seòl.

Falaichear cladach na trioblaid
Le bhoghachan is tiùrr a' bhròin
Is buailidh an tonn gun bhristeadh
Mu m' chasan le suathadh sròil.

Ciamar nach do mhair an reothairt
By bhuidhe dhomh na do na h-eòin
Agus a chaill mi a cobhair
'S i tràghadh boinn air bhoinne bròin?

73

Spring-tide

Again and again when I am broken
my thought comes on you when you were young,
and the incomprehensible sea fills
with flood-tide and a thousand sails.

The shore of trouble is hidden
with its reefs and its wrack of sorrow,
and the unbreaking wave strikes
about my feet with a rubbing of silk.

How did the spring-tide not last,
that was more golden to me than to the birds,
and how did I lose its succour
ebbing drop by drop of grief?

(The reference in the last verse is to Reothairt nan Eun, the
Spring-tide of the Birds, at the time of the return of migrants.)

SYDNEY TREMAYNE (b. 1912)

Small Boy and Lighthouse

You, little rugged boy without seat to your trousers,
Your senses pinned to a string, your boots hanging over the harbour,
Remember, when you are older, the green sea rocking,
The black sea knocking the ships;
Remember the taut ropes groaning, the lift and suck of the hulls,
The smell of the herring boxes, the bright scales stuck to the jetty,
The sequin scales on your hands, that you wipe on your trousers.
Remember the swearing gulls and the gannets diving,
The cormorants crucified; remember the rust-caked dredger,
The coal truck swung from a crane, and the dust, and the thunder.
Remember the huge night also, with zigzag on slow water
Of yellow and red lights tangling, and how from darkness
A white flash, sharp as a pin, pulled out an island.

Outpost in Winter

Mist lines the ground, a tracing of fine snow.
The field's unsettled as a sea
Through which the moles like whales come up to blow.
The tree that swims in grey might be
A spineless weed buoyed up to reach the air.
Silence is deep. Night shrinks; there is no star.

We two adrift in winter share with birds
Confinement of the dark that comes,
Silence banked upon silence, stranding words.
Outside, unsleeping stillness thrums
To our intense listening like a heart
Echoing back from depths not on the chart.

Something that needs a refuge scrapes the eaves.
Birdfoot or ratfoot stirs the straw.
There is not wind to move the fallen leaves
For we should hear it softly draw
Ripples along the darkness: nothing at all
Except what seeks the shelter of a wall.

This is the arc of winter bending through
Its longest circuit from the light.
And we among the creatures, few,
That have a stake here, riding out the night
Feel the slow shift of time like a great strength
Reaching us up against our tether's length.

DOUGLAS YOUNG (b. 1913)

Winter Pool

The pool in the dark rocks reflects the sky no longer,
    No more ripples with wind, nor mirrors the sunlight flicker
Through air-swept fronds of fern. The ice nightly stronger
    Settles upon it tight, each morning tighter and thicker.

Brown and flaccid now the polypodies dangle,
   Mahogany-red beech-leaves freeze to the ice-cover;
Under the clear black ice the pondweed tresses tangle,
   And black-green rotting buds of the waterlilies hover.

Out of the litter of leaves in those slimy dull recesses
   Three goldfish glide, torpidly gaping and squinting,
To patrol their gloomy world that the prisoning ice compresses.
   I come daily and watch, and am glad at their golden glinting.

Last Lauch

The Minister said it wald dee,
   the cypress buss I plantit.
But the buss grew til a tree,
   naething dauntit.

It's growan, stark and heich,
   derk and straucht and sinister,
kirkyairdie-like and dreich.
   But whaur's the Minister?

G. S. FRASER (b. 1914)

Hometown Elegy
(for Aberdeen in Spring)

Glitter of mica at the windy corners,
Tar in the nostrils, under blue lamps budding
Like bubbles of glass and the blue buds of a tree,
Night-shining shopfronts, or the sleek sun flooding
The broad abundant dying sprawl of the Dee:
For these and for their like my thoughts are mourners
That yet shall stand, though I come home no more,
Gas works, white ballroom, and the red brick baths
And salmon nets along a mile of shore,

Or beyond the municipal golf-course, the moorland paths
And the country lying quiet and full of farms.
This is the shape of a land that outlasts a strategy
And is not to be taken with rhetoric or arms.
Or my own room, with a dozen books on the bed
(Too late, still musing what I mused, I lie
And read too lovingly what I have read),
Brantome, Spinoza, Yeats, the bawdy and wise,
Continuing their interminable debate,
With no conclusion, they conclude too late,
When their wisdom has fallen like a grey pall on my eyes.
Syne we maun part, there sall be nane remeid—
Unless my country is my pride, indeed,
Or I can make my town that homely fame
That Byron has, from boys in Carden Place,
Struggling home with books to midday dinner,
For whom he is not the romantic sinner,
The careless writer, the tormented face,
The hectoring bully or the noble fool,
But, just like Gordon or like Keith, a name:
A tall, proud statue at the Grammar School.

Meditation of a Patriot

The posters show my country blonde and green,
Like some sweet siren, but the travellers know
How dull the shale sky is, the airs how keen,
And how our boorish manners freeze like snow.
Romantic Scotland was an emigrant,
Half-blooded, and escaped from sullen weather.
Here, we toss off a dram to drown a cough
And whisky has the trade-mark of the heather.
My heart yearns southwards as the shadows slant,
I wish I were an exile and I rave:
    With Byron and with Lermontov
    Romantic Scotland's in the grave.

In Glasgow, that damned sprawling evil town,
I interview a vulgar editor,
Who, brawny, self-made, looks me up and down
And seems to wonder what my sort is for.
Do I write verse? Ah, man, but that is bad . . .
And, too polite, I fawn upon this tough,
But when I leave him, O my heart is sad.
He sings alone who in this province sings.
I kick a lamp-post, and in drink I rave:
    With Byron and with Lermontov
    Romantic Scotland's in the grave.

In the far islands to the north and west
Mackenzie and MacDiarmid have their peace.
St. Andrews soothes that critic at her breast
Whose polished verse ne'er gave his soul release.
I have no islands and no ancient stone,
Only the sugary granite glittering crisp
Pleases the eye, but turns affection off,
Hard rhetoric, that never learned to lisp.
This town has beauty, but I walk alone
And to the flat and sallow sands I rave:
    With Byron and with Lermontov
    Romantic Scotland's in the grave.

The Death of My Grandmother

There's little personal grief in a quiet old death:
Grief for a landscape dying in our heads,
Knowing how London melts us to her style.
What if she got those touches in her talk
(The half-impression of a scene that had
Flowed in her youthful blood and set as bone)
From phrases in some novel by John Buchan?
A memory is other than the words for it:
Persistence was her gift, not literature,
A character no town could penetrate,
Not Glasgow's sprawl, nor London's repetitions—
No more that landscape now: no more the old
Books in the glass case, and the box bed
I half remember as a boy in Glasgow:

Caithness enclosed within a house in Glasgow,
Glasgow enclosed in London: time in time,
The past within the past, parentheses.
In laying her to rest, it is as if
We folded up with her brown age a landscape,
A ribbed and flat and rocky map of duty
That is the northern edge of every island
Where pleasure flowers only in the swollen south:
Mourn character that could persist so long
Where softer personality dies young.

These lights and glimpses lost now: only bones,
Shapes of our heads, only the arguing voice,
In a foreign milieu the improvised fine manners.

Think of these rock-stacks in the stoney Orkneys
That, toppling, stand improbably for years,
The sea persisting at them: and at last,
Boys' bricks, they crash on the untidy beach.
So with her piled and uncemented past:
Its tottering tower seemed out of the tide's reach.
Time merely fretted at the base. No more
Of all the colour of her years was hers
Than brown rock's is blue sea's. O travellers,
Who take the stain of Time, as I have done,
Expose your fluctuations to the sun:
Yet, for such stony virtue, spare your tears.

R. CROMBIE SAUNDERS (b. 1914)

The Empty Glen

Time ticks away the centre of my pride
Emptying its glen of cattle, crops, and song,
Till its deserted headlands are alone
Familiar with the green uncaring tide.

What gave this land to gradual decay?
The rocky field where plovers make their nest
Now undisturbed had once the soil to raise
A happy people, but from day to day

The hamlets failed, the young men sought the towns,
Bewildered age looked from the cottage door
Upon the wreck of all they'd laboured for,
The rotting gate, the bracken on the downs;

And wondered if the future was so black
The children would have stayed but did not dare,
Who might, they hoped, be happy where they are.
And wondered, Are they ever coming back?

RUTHVEN TODD (b. 1914)

Personal History: For My Son

O my heart is the unlucky heir of the ages
And my body is unwillingly the secret agent
Of my ancestors; those content with their wages
From history: the Cumberland Quaker whose gentle
Face was framed with lank hair to hide the ears
Cropped as a punishment for his steadfast faith,
The Spanish lady who had seen the pitch lake's broth
In the West Indian island, and the Fife farmers
To whom the felted barley meant a winter's want.

My face presents my history, and its sallow skin
Is parchment for the Edinburgh lawyer's deed:
To have and hold in trust, as feeofee therein
Until such date as the owner shall have need
Thereof. My brown eyes are jewels I cannot pawn,
And my long lip once curled beside an Irish bog,
My son's whorled ear was once my father's, then mine;
I am the map of a campaign, each ancestor has his flag
Marking an advance or a retreat. I am their seed.

As I write I look at the five fingers of my hand,
Each with its core of nacre bone, and rippled nails;
Turn to the palm and the traced unequal lines that end
In death—only at the tips my ancestry fails—
The dotted swirls are original and are my own:
Look at this fringed polyp which I daily use
And ask its history, ask to what grave abuse
It has been put: perhaps it curled about the stone
Of Cain. At least it has known much of evil.

And perhaps as much of good, been tender
When tenderness was needed, and been firm
On occasion, and in its past been free of gender,
Been the hand of a mother holding the warm
Impress of the child against her throbbing breast,
Been cool to the head inflamed in fever,
Sweet and direct in contact with a lover.
O in its cupped and fluted shell lies all the past,
My fingers close about the crash of history's storm.

In the tent of night I hear the voice of Calvin
Expending his hatred of the world in icy winds;
Man less than red ant beneath the towering mountain,
And God a troll more fearful than the feudal lords;
The Huguenots in me, flying Saint Bartholomew's Day,
Are in agreement with all this, and their resentful hate
Flames brighter than the candles on an altar, the grey
Afternoon is lit by Catherine wheels of terror, the street
Drinks blood, and pity is death before their swords.

The cantilever of my bones acknowledges the architect,
My father, to whom always the world was a mystery
Concealed in the humped base of a bottle, one solid fact
To set against the curled pages and the tears of history.
I am a Border keep, a croft and a solicitor's office,
A country rectory, a farm and a drawing board:
In me, as in so many, the past has stowed its miser's hoard,
Won who knows where nor with what loaded dice.
When my blood pulses it is their blood I feel hurry.

These forged me, the latest link in a fertile chain,
With ends that run so far that my short sight
Cannot follow them, nor can my weak memory claim

Acquaintance with the earliest shackle. In my height
And breadth I hold my history, and then my son
Holds my history in his small body and the history of another,
Who for me has no contact but that of flesh, his mother.
What I make now I make, indeed, from the unknown,
A blind man spinning furiously in the web of night.

SYDNEY GOODSIR SMITH (b. 1915)

Elegy VI: What Wey Suld I

I

What wey suld I, my hairt's luve,
Scrieve ye mair?
Hae ye no had a thrave o' sangs
Frae me ere nou?
—And ye wad answer:
Why indeed?
Hae ye no had a haill beuk-fu
O' sangs frae me?
What need is there
For scrievin mair?
—And ye wad answer:
What indeed?

II

And trulie there are maitters o' great moment
Abraid the day.
Aa the great michtie
In their great seats are warslan
For anither cushion maybe
Or mair licht,
Or the table

wey—way   suld—should   scrieve—write   thrave—sheaf
haill—whole   beuk-fu—book-full   maitters—matters   abraid—abroad
michtie—mighty   warslan—wrestling   mair—more

A wee thing nearer til the great hand,
      Or mair cigars, or better anes,
          Brandy, usquebae
              Or what hae ye.
And, tae, theres ithers maist important questions
          For a bard—
          'The Antennae o' the Race,'
          'The Unacknowledged Legislators,'
          'Sperits o' the Time,' and sae furth,
As some enthusiasts hae observed
Frae time til time in moments o' exaltatioun
              Or euphoria
Sequant til the drinkin o' wine maistlikelie
And the saft hand o' a suppositatit virgin
      (Government Guarantee for Foreign Envoys)
          Caller on their fevered powes
Wi promises o' yet further exaltatiouns
Likelie til accume gif but they play
Their stack o' aces eydentlie—
En effet, maist serious maitters
O' great argument to consider maist earnestlie
              And seriouslie.

          This is nae time for lassies' fykes!
              I'm sure ye'll gree.
          And Echo dulie answers:
                  Gree!

III

And truth it is
There was a day I micht
Hae thocht there micht
Be sunkots intil't.
But nou a lassie's flegmageeries
And my ain tae, admittedlie,
Tak aa my time, aa thocht,
Aa dwaums and aa activitie.

usquebae—whisky   tae—too ithers—others   maistlikelie—most likely
saft—soft   caller—cool   powe—head   wi—with   accume—accumulate
gif—if   eydentlie—carefully   fykes—whims   gree—agree
thocht—thought   sunkots—something   intil't—in it
flegmageeries—fancies   aa—all   dwaums—dreams

For I was born excessive, Scorpio,
In aathing and in luve;
Eneuch's no near as guid's a feast til me,
The middle airt, the Gowden Mean,
Has little recommandan hit
As far as I can see,
And in the hairt's affectioun
I find nae exceptioun.

The warld and aa its ills
Are, certes, unco eerie,
But the nou til me they're nil
Forenent a lassie's flegmageerie.

Tho Scotland's saul is brairan
As the saul o' Europe dwynes
And tho I dout there's neer a Czar
Can ding us doun for aye—
Yet aa sic speculatiouns flee
Intil the mirkest airts
O' a zero o' ariditie
Gin the blind bairn jags my hairt
    By nicht and day
Wi' a lassie's whims and whams,
    A lassie's yea and nay.

        (A maist reprehensible estate
        O' affairs, I maun admit.)

aathing—everything   eneuch—enough   airt—area   gowden—golden
certes—certainly   unco—very   eerie—dismal   the nou—now
forenent—compared with   saul—soul   brairan—sprouting
dwynes—dwindles   dout—doubt   ding—knock   doun—down
mirkest—darkest   bairn—child   maun—must

Elegy XII: Orpheus

I

Wi sang aa birds and beasts could I owrecome,
Aa men and wemen o' the mapamound subdue,
    The flouers o' the fields,
Rocks and trees, boued doun to hear my leid,
Gurlie waters rase upon the land to mak
    A throwgang for my feet.
I was the potent prince o' ballatrie,
My clarsach opened portes whareer I thocht to gang,
    My fleean sangs mair ramsh nor wine
At Beltane, Yule or Hogmanay
    Made wud the clans o' men—
There wasna my maik upon the yerth
    (Why suld I no admit the fack?)
A hero, demi-god, my kinrik was the hairt,
    The passions and the saul,
        Sic was my pouer.
—Anerlie my ain sel I couldna bend.

    'He was his ain warst enemie,'
    As the auld untentit bodachs say—
    My hairt, a leopard, ruthless, breme,
    Gilravaged far and near
Seekan sensatiouns, passions that wad wauken
    My Muse whan she was lollish.
No seendil the hairt was kinnelt like a forest-bleeze. . . .
I was nae maister o' my ain but thirlit
    Serf til his ramskeerie wants
—And yet I hained but ane i the hairt's deepest hairt.

mapamound—map of the world   boued—bowed   doun—down
leid—song   gurlie—angry   rase—rose   throwgang—thoroughfare
ballatrie—ballad making   clarsach—a small harp   fleean—passionate
mair—more   ramsh—intoxicating   wud—mad   maik—equal
yerth—earth   fack—fact   kinrik—kingdom   hert—heart   saul—soul
sic—such   pouer—power   anerlie—only   ain sel—own self
untentit—uncared for   bodach—old man   breme—fierce
gilravaged—behave riotously   wauken—waken   lollish—lazy, idle
seendil—seldom   kinnelt—kindled   forest-bleeze—forest-blaze
thirlit—bound   ramskeerie—lustful, abandoned   hained—cherished
ane—one

She, maist leefou, leesome leddy
　　—Ochone, ochone, Euridicie—
Was aye the queen of Orpheus' hairt, as I kent weill,
And wantan her my life was feckless drinkin,
Weirdless, thieveless dancin,
　　　　Singin, gangrellin.
　　　　　　—And nou she's gane.

II

The jalous gods sae cast my weird that she
Was reift intil the Shades throu my negleck.
　　I, daffan in the shaws and pools
　　　　Wi the water-lassies,
　　　　Riggish, ree, and aye as fain
　　For lemanrie as Orpheus was,
I never kent o' her stravaigin,
　　　　Lane and dowie in the fields;
Nor that yon Aristaeus loed my queyne.
　　It was fleean him she deed
But yet was my negleck that did the deed;
Neither was I by her to proteck
　　Frae the dernit serpent's bane
Green and secret in the raff gerss liggan
—I was her daith as she was life til me,
　　　　Tho I was feckless born and lemanous
Yet she was mair nor aa the daft ree nymphs
　　O' wuid and burn til me
　　　　—Yet it was I
　　That flung Euridicie
　　The aipple o' my bruckle ee
　　　　Til yon far bourne
Frae whilk, they said, there's can be nae retourn.
　　　　'Quhair art thow gane, my luve euridicess?'

maist—most　　leefou—loving　　leesome—beloved　　leddy—lady
ochone—alas　　feckless—purposeless　　weirdless—aimless
thieveless—feeble　　gangrellin—wandering　　gane—gone
jalous—jealous　　weird—fate　　reift—snatched　　intil—into
negleck—neglect　　daffan—sporting　　riggish—randy
ree—lecherous　　lemanrie—sensuality　　stravaigin—wandering
lane—lonely　　dowie—sad　　loed—loved　　queyne—girl
fleean—flying from　　proteck—protect　　dernit—hidden　　bane—poison
raff—rank　　gerss—grass　　liggan—lying　　lemanous—amorous
daft—silly　　wuid—wood　　aipple—apple　　bruckle—brittle
frae whilk—from which　　gane—gone

III

Ye ken the tale, hou, wi my lute
    I doungaed amang the Shades
(Gray mauchie Hades, lichtless airt)
And Pluto and the damned stude round
    And grat, hearan my sang;
Hou, haean wan her manumissioun
Frae the Profund Magnifico,
I, cryan her name, socht and fand my luve
    Amang thae wearie shadaws,
    Yet tint her in the end.
        For her a second daith,
        For me a second shame.

        (The sycophantic gods, ulyied and curlit,
        Reclynan in the bar on bricht Olympus.
        Soupan their meridian, outbocked
        Their lauchter like a tourbilloun
        At this the latest ploy o' Zeus
        The Caird, the Conjuror, the aye-bydan
        Favourite and darlin o' them aa,
        The Wide Boy—*ex officio!*
                    —The Charlatan!)

She stummelt on a bourach, outcried 'Orpheus!'
—Een, what wey were ye no blind?
—Lugs, what wey were ye no deif?
—Hairt, what wey were ye no cauld as ice?
—Limbs, what wey were ye no pouerless?
—Harns, what wey did ye no haud the owerance?

        (And Jupiter, in order til extraict
        The maist exquisite quintessence
        O' the succulence o' his wee ploy
        And wi his infantile perfectit sense

doungaed—went down   amang—among   mauchie—dark
lichtless—without light   grat—wept   haean—having   wan—won
socht—sought   fand—found   tint—lost   daith—death
ulyied—oiled   curlit—curled   soupan—supping   outbocked—poured out
lauchter—laughter   ploy—game   caird—rogue   aye-bydan—everlasting
stummelt—stumbled   bourach—pile of stones   een—eyes   lugs—ears
deif—deaf   hairt—heart   pouerless—powerless   harns—brains
haud—hold   owerance—authority

O' the dramatic, kept this impeccabil
And maikless agonie,
As a *bonne-bouche*, til the end.)

We werena ten yairds frae the bank o' Styx
The ferryin o' whilk was luve and libertie
    —No ten yairds awa!
Our braith was hechlan and our een
    Glaizie-glentit wi the joy
    Of our twa-fauld deliverance—
And then Jove strak wi serpent subtletie.
    Euridicie stummelt.

        (Lauchter cracked abune. Jupiter leuch!
          —And richtlie sae!
        Och, gie the gods their due
        They ken what they're about.
           —The Sleekans!)

She stummelt. I heard her cry. And hairt ruled heid again.
—What hairt could eer refuse, then, siccan a plea?
    I turned—
        And wi neer a word,
           In silence,
Her een yet bricht wi the joy o' resurrectioun,
She soomed awa afore my een intil a skimmeran wraith
And for a second and last time was tint for aye
    Amang the gloams and haars o' Hell
        —Throu my ain twafauld treacherie!
        'Quhair art thow gane, my luve euridicess?'

IV

Sinsyne I haena plucked a note
    Nor made a word o' a sang,
The clarsach, and the lyre, the lute,
    'The aiten reed',

maikless—matchless   whilk—which   braith—breath   hechlan—panting
glaizie-glentit—glittering   twa-fauld—two-fold   strak—struck
lauchter—laughter   abune—above   leuch—laughed   richtlie—rightly
sae—so   sleekans—crafty ones   siccan—such   bricht—bright
soomed—swam   awa—away   intil—into   skimmeran—shimmering
tint—lost   gloams—twilights   sinsyne—since then   haena—have not
aiten—oaten

Byde untuned in a yerdit kist.
My taiblets aa are broke, my pens brunt,
> The howff sees me nocht
> Nor the lassies in the glen.
> The hairt in my bosom's deid
> > For Euridicie is deid
And it was I that did the double deed,
> Twice-cursit Orpheus!

I gang to jyne her in the skuggie airt,
A convene fou o dreid for Orpheus' hairt.

> Aa this will happen aa again,
> Monie and monie a time again.
> > > *(Explicit Orpheus.)*

byde—remain   yerdit—buried   kist—chest   taiblets—tablets
brunt—burnt   howff—tavern   deid—dead   jyne—join
skuggie—shadowy   airt—part   fou—full   dreid—dread   monie—many

GEORGE CAMPBELL HAY (b. 1915)

The Old Fisherman

Greet the bights that gave me shelter,
they will hide me no more with the horns of their forelands.
I peer in a haze, my back is stooping;
my dancing days for fishing are over.

The shoot that was straight in the wood withers,
the bracken shrinks red in the rain and shrivels,
the eyes that would gaze in the sun waver;
my dancing days for fishing are over.

The old boat must seek the shingle,
her wasting side hollow the gravel,
the hand that shakes must leave the tiller;
my dancing days for fishing are over.

The sea was good night and morning,
the winds were friends, the calm was kindly—
the snow seeks the burn, the brown fronds scatter;
my dancing days for fishing are over.

The Auld Hunter

From the Gaelic of George Campbell Hay
(Scots version by Hugh MacDiarmid)

Eild comes owre me like a yoke on my craig,
A girn roon' my feet, the lourd and the chill.
Betwixt my sicht and the licht it comes,
It comes betwixt the deed and the will.

This is the thing that warps the sapling
And sets its knife to the aipple's root,
But the warst deed o' a' its spite has been
To filch the hill frae under my foot.

My narrow gun and the paths o' the cruach
Eild has stown, wha's deef and heeds nae grief;
My hand and my foot, this Blear-eyed's stown them
And a' my cheer, like a hertless thief.

But gin Eild were a man that hauns could grapple
And I could come on him secretly
Up there on the hill when naebody passes
Certes! Grass 'ud be trampled or he gat free!

eild—age   craig—neck   girn—grouse   roon'—round   lourd—weight
sicht—sight   licht—light   aipple—apple   cruach—mountain
stown—stolen   deef—deaf   nae—no   gin—if   hauns—hands

W. S. GRAHAM (b. 1917)

From

The Night Fishing

We are at the hauling then hoping for it
The hard slow haul of a net white with herring
Meshed hard. I haul, using the boat's cross-heave
We've started, holding fast as we rock back,
Taking slack as we go to. The day rises brighter
Over us and the gulls rise in a wailing scare
From the nearest net-floats. And the unfolding water
Mingles its dead.

Now better white I can say what's better sighted,
The white net flashing under the watched water,
The near net dragging back with the full belly
Of a good take certain, so drifted easy
Slow down on us or us hauled up upon it
Curved in a garment down to thicker fathoms.
The hauling nets come in sawing the gunwale
With herring scales.

The air bunches to a wind and roused sea-cries.
The weather moves and stoops high over us and
There the forked tern, where my look's whetted on distance,
Quarters its hunting sea. I haul slowly
Inboard the drowning flood as into memory,
Braced at the breathside in my net of nerves.
We haul and drift them home. The winds slowly
Turn round on us and

Gather towards us with dragging weights of water
Sleekly swelling across the humming sea
And gather heavier. We haul and hold and haul
Well the bright chirpers home, so drifted whitely
All a blinding garment out of the grey water.
And, hauling hard in the drag, the nets come in,
The headrope a sore pull and feeding its brine
Into our hacked hands.

Over the gunwale over into our deep lap
The herring come in, staring from their scales,
Fruitful as our deserts would have it out of
The deep and shifting seams of water. We haul
Against time fallen ill over the gathering
Rush of the sea together. The calms dive down.
The strident kingforked airs roar in their shell.
We haul the last

Net home and the last tether off the gathering
Run of the started sea. And then was the first
Hand at last lifted getting us swung against
Into the homing quarter, running that white grace
That sails me surely ever away from home.
And we hold into it as it moves down on
Us running white on the hull heeled to light.
Our bow heads home

Into the running blackbacks soaring us loud
High up in open arms of the towering sea.
The steep bow heaves, hung on these words, towards
What words your lonely breath blows out to meet it.
It is the skilled keel itself knowing its own
Fathoms it further moves through, with us there
Kept in its common timbers, yet each of us
Unwound upon

By a lonely behaviour of the all common ocean.
I cried headlong from my dead. The long rollers,
Quick on the crests and shirred with fine foam,
Surge down then sledge their green tons weighing dead
Down on the shuddered deck-boards. And shook off
All that white arrival upon us back to falter
Into the waking spoil and to be lost in
The mingling world.

So we were started back over that sea we
Had worked widely all fish-seasons and over
Its shifting grounds, yet now risen up into
Such humours, I felt like a farmer tricked to sea.
For it sailed sore against us. It grew up
To black banks that crossed us. It stooped, beaked.
Its brine burnt us. I was chosen and given.
It rose as risen

Treachery becomes myself, to clip me amorously
Off from all common breath. Those fires burned
Sprigs of the foam and branching tines of water.
It rose so white, soaring slowly, up
On us, then broke, down on us. It became a mull
Against our going and unfastened under us and
Curdled from the stern. It shipped us at each blow.
The brute weight

Of the living sea wrought us, yet the boat sleeked lean
Into it, upheld by the whole sea-brunt heaved,
And hung on the swivelling tops. The tiller raised
The siding tide to wrench us and took a good
Ready hand to hold it. Yet we made a seaway
And minded all the gear was fast, and took
Our spell at steering. And we went keeled over
The streaming sea.

See how, like an early self, it's loath to leave
And stares from the scuppers as it swirls away
To be clenched up. What a great width stretches
Farsighted away fighting in its white straits
On either bow, but bears up our boat on all
Its plaiting strands. This wedge driven in
To the twisting water, we rode. The bow shores
The long rollers.

The keel climbs and, with screws spinning out of their bite,
We drive down into the roar of the great doorways,
Each time almost to overstay, but start
Up into again the yelling gale and hailing
Shot of the spray. Yet we should have land
Soon marking us out of this thick distance and
How far we're in. Who is that poor sea-scholar,
Braced in his hero,

Lost in his book of storms there? It is myself.
So he who died is announced. This mingling element
Gives up myself. Words travel from what they once
Passed silence with. Here, in this intricate death,
He goes as fixed on silence as ever he'll be.
Leave him, nor cup a hand to shout him out
Of that, his home. Or, if you would, O surely
There is no word,

There is not any to go over that.
It is now as always this difficult air
We look towards each other through. And is there
Some singing look or word or gesture of grace
Or naked wide regard from the encountered face,
Goes ever true through the difficult air?
Each word speaks its own speaker to his death.
And we saw land

At last marked on the tenting mist and we could
Just make out the ridge running from the north
To the Black Rosses, and even mark the dark hint
Of Skeer well starboard. Now inside the bight
The sea was loosening and the screws spun steadier
Beneath us. We still shipped the blown water but
It broke white, not green weight caved in on us.
In out of all

That forming and breaking sea we came on the long
Swell close at last inshore with the day grey
With mewing distances and mist. The rocks rose
Waving their lazy friendly weed. We came in
Moving now by the world's side. And O the land lay
Just as we knew it well all along that shore
Akin to us with each of its dear seamarks. And lay
Like a mother.

We came in, riding steady in the bay water,
A sailing pillar of gulls, past the cockle strand.
And springing teal came out of the long sand. We
Moved under the soaring land sheathed in fair water
In that time's morning grace. I uttered that place
And left each word I was. The quay-heads lift up
To pass us in. These sea-worked measures end now.
And this element

Ends as we move off from its formal instant.
Now he who takes my place continually anew
Speaks me thoroughly perished into another.
And the quay opened its arms. I heard the sea
Close on him gently swinging on oiled hinges.
Moored here, we cut the motor quiet. He that
I'm not lies down. Men shout. Words break. I am
My fruitful share.

MAURICE LINDSAY (b. 1918)

On Seeing a Picture o Johann Christian Fischer in the National Gallery, Edinburgh

Johann Christian Fischer? Mm—the face is kindly,
the wig weil-snod, the features firmly set,
as leanan on a harpsichord by Albrecht,
wi quill in haun you scrieve a menuet.

weil-snod—well-trimmed   leanan—leaning   scrieve—write

The feet sae carefully crossed tae shaw the buckl't shuin,
gimp hose and curly cravat o white lace,
the fiddle on the chair, the music heaped—
the hail, a glisk o eighteenth Century grace!

Gin ony o your stately airs and tunefu dances
that kittle't pouther't duchesses lang syne,
culd tinkle oot o Albrecht's yalla keyboard,
maist folk 'ud luik at you a second time.

But aa is dusty silence, like the derk ahint you,
and e'en your notes are naethin but a blur;
the background, fu o shaddaws, seems tae draw you
tae hap you in its aa-embracan slur.

Yet there you staun oot still, by Gainsborough made immortal,
as gin sic fame was shairly jist your due—
a perfect shell upon the shore left strandit,
a piece for antiquarians tae view.

shaw—show   shuin—shoes   gimp—neat   hail—whole   glisk—glimpse
gin—if   ony—any   kittle't—tickled   pouther't—powdered
lang syne—long ago   yalla—yellow   derk—dark   hap—cover
slur—scorn   staun—stand   oot—out   shairly—surely

At Hans Christian Andersen's Birthplace, Odense, Denmark

Sunlight folds back pages of quiet shadows
against the whitewashed walls of his birthplace.
                                        Tourists move
through crowded antiseptic rooms and ponder
what row after row of glass-cased papers ought to prove.

Somehow the long-nosed gangling boy who was only
at home in fairy-land, has left no clues.
The tinder-box of Time we rub
answers us each the way we choose.

95

For kings have now no daughters left for prizes.
Swineherds must remain swineherds; not a spell
can make the good man prince; psychiatrists
have dredged up wonder from the wishing well.

The whole of his terrible, tiny world might be
dismissed as a beautiful madman's dream, but that each
                                        of us knows
whenever we move out from the warmth of our loneliness
we may be wearing the Emperor's new clothes.

School Prizegiving

The voice rose out of his enormous paunch
reverberent with wisdom rounded there
since he had stood, a sliver of himself,
with boys like these in some lost otherwhere

innumerable platitudes away.
And yet, for all its width, the voice was small,
smooth-feathered still, cock-crested in success
that time had caponed, centre of the hall.

And as his little meanings strutted out
in preening words, the eager fledgling boys
who listened must have wondered if they too
might one day make the same wing-beating noise

to keep their courage up, their run of years
inexplicably fouled, their hopeful hastes
turned back upon themselves; each still so sure
he'd force his way beyond these middle wastes . . .

And I, aware how satisfaction breaks
against its realisation, and how thick
the darkness gathers, caught myself, ashamed,
half-murmuring: 'Their prizes, masters. Quick!'

Farm Widow

She moved among the sour smell of her hens' droppings,
her cheeks rubbed to a polish, her skirts bustled
with decent pride; alone since the day the tractor
hauled itself up the field on the hill and toppled

her man away from her. Around her feet
her daughter played, the face of innocence puckered
with the solemn self-importance of being alone
in a grown-up world; her friends, the hens that speckled

her mother's allotment. Some of the weekly folk
who came to buy their eggs, watched her counting
their change from the money smooth in her purse, had given her
silent pity, then sensed that she wasn't wanting

in anything they could offer; that she seemed
like one whom life had used too soon for writing
some sort of purpose with, her gestures economies
spelling completeness; gone beyond our waiting

for times and places to happen, beyond the will,
to where time and place lie colourless and still.

Picking Apples

Apple time, and the trees bristle with fruit.
My children climb the bent, half-sapping branches
to where the apples, cheeked with the hectic flush
of Autumn, hang. The children bark their haunches

and lean on the edge of their balance. The apples are out
of reach; so they shake the tree. Through a tussle of leaves and
    laughter
the apples thud down; thud on the orchard grasses
in rounded, grave finality, each one after

97

the other dropping; the muffled sound of them dropping
like suddenly hearing the beats of one's own heart
falling away, as if shaken by some storm
as localised as this. Loading them into the cart,

the sweet smell of their bruises moist in the sun,
their skins' bloom tacky against the touch,
I experience fulfilment, suddenly aware
of some ripe, wordless answer, knowing no such

answers exist; only questions, questions, the beating years,
the dropped apples . . . the kind of touch and go
that poetry makes satisfactions of;
reality, with nothing more to show

than a brush of branches, time and the apples falling,
and shrill among the leaves, children impatiently calling.

Aged Four

Alone beside himself, head-in-air
he wanders gently through a fading season,
almost for the last time aware
of how a moment feels, before the lesion

of growing into thought begins to hurt;
the falling burn turn into a complaint
it can't communicate; earth on the hands be dirt
that rubs a sudden scolding up; each feint

the wind boxes the trees with, trace a why
nobody answers; rain be more than wet;
clouds that unfold each other, shape a sky
forecasting portent. Head-in-air, and yet

reluctant to come in, he stands and bawls,
sensing from how much loss his mother calls.

TOM SCOTT (b. 1918)

Auld Sanct-Aundrians—Brand the Builder

On winter days, about the gloamin hour,
Whan the knock on the college touer
Is chappan lowsin-time,
And ilk mason packs his mell and tools awa
Ablow his banker, and bien forenenst the waa
The labourer haps the lave o the lime
Wi soppan secks, to keep it frae a frost, or faa
o suddent snaw
Duran the nicht,
And scrawnie craws flap in the shell-green licht
Towards yon bane-bare rickle o trees
That heeze
Up on the knowe abuin the toun,
And the red goun
Is happan mony a student frae the snell nor-easter,
Malcolm Brand, the maister,
Seean the last hand throu the yett
Afore he bars and padlocks it,
Taks ae look round his stourie yaird
Whaur chunks o stane are liggan
Like the ruins o some auld-farrant biggin:
Picks a skelf out o his baerd,
Scliffs his tacketty buits, and syne
Clunters hamelins doun the wyn'.

Auld Sanct-Aundrians—Old St. Andrians   knock—clock
chappan—striking   lowsin-time—knocking-off time   ilk—every
mell—mason's mallet   ablow—below   banker—hewing table
bien—snug   forenenst—against   waa—wall   haps—covers   lave—remainder
soppan—soaking   secks—sacks   faa—fall   bane-bare—bone-bare
rickle—skeletal stack   heeze—rise   knowe—knoll   abuin—above
toun—town   goun—gown   snell—bitter   yett—gate   afore—before
stourie—dusty   yaird—yard   stane—stone   liggan—lying
auld-farrant—old-fashioned   biggin—building   skelf—splinter
baerd—beard   scliffs—scuffs   buits—boots   syne—then
clunters—moves heavily   hamelins—homewards   wyn'—wynd (lane)

Alang the shore,
The greinan white sea-owsen ramp and roar.
The main street echoes back his clinkan fuit-faas
Frae its waas,
Whaur owre the kerb and causeys yellow licht
Presses back the mirk nicht
As shop-fronts flüde the pavin-stanes in places,
Like the peintit faces
Whures pit on, or actresses,—ay, or meenisters—
To plaese their several customers.
But aye the nordren nicht, cauld as rumour,
Taks command,
Chills the toun wi his militarie humour,
And plots his map o starns wi deadly hand.

Doun by the sea,
Murns the white swaw owre the wrack ayebydanlie.

Stoupan throu the anvil pend
Gaes Brand,
And owre the coort wi the twa-three partan creels,
The birss air fu
o the smell o the sea, and fish, and meltit glue,
Draws up at his door, and syne,
Hawkan his craig afore he gangs in ben,
Gies a bit scrape at the grater wi his heels.

The kail-pat on the hob is hotteran fu
o the usual hash o Irish stew,
And by the grate, a red-haired bewtie frettit thin,
His wife is kaain a spurtle round.

---

alang—along   greinan—yearning   sea-owsen—sex oxen (sea horses)
ramp—rampage   clinkan—clinking   fuit-faas—foot-falls
causeys—cobble-stones   mirk nicht—dark night
pavin-stanes—paving stones   peintit—painted   whures—whores
plaese—please   nordren—northern   cauld—cold   starns—stars
doun—down   murns—mourns   swaw—wave   wrack—sea-weed
ayebydanlie—everlastingly   stoupan—stooping   pend—arch leading to a close
coort—court   twa-three—two or three   partans—edible crabs   creels—basket
birss—sharp   fu—full   hawkan his craig—clearing his throat
ben—to the furthermost part of the house   kail-pat—kail-pot   frettit—worr
kaain—driving   spurtle—wooden rod for stirring

He swaps his buits for his baffies but a sound.
The twa-three bairnies ken to mak nae din
Whan faither's in,
And sit on creepies round about.
Brand gies a muckle yawn, and howks his paper out.

Tither side the fire,
The kettle sings like a telephone wire.

   'Lord, for what we are about to receive
   Help us to be truly thankful—Aimen—
   Wumman, ye've pit ingans in't again.'
   'Gae wa ye auld hypocrite!
   Thank the Lord for your maet, syne grue at it!'

Wi chowks drawn ticht in a speakless sconner
He glowers on her:
Syne on the quate and straucht-faced bairns:
Faulds his paper doun by his eatin-airns,
And, till the loud tick-tockin o the knock,
Sups, and reads, wi nae ither word nor look.

The warld outside
Like a lug-held sea-shell, roars wi the rinnan tide.

The supper owre, Brand redds up for the nicht.
Aiblins there's a schedule for to price,
Or somethin nice
On at the picters—sacont hoose—
Or some poleetical meetin wants his licht,
Or aiblins, wi him t-total aa his life,
No able to seek the pub to flee the wife,

swaps—exchanges   buits—boots   baffies—slippers   but—without
creepies—stools   howks—digs   tither—the other   ingans—onions
gae wa—go away   maet—food   syne—then
grue—shudder (*here*—complain)   chowks—cheeks   ticht—tight
speakless—speechless   sconner—repulsion   glowers—glares
quate—quiet   straucht-faced—straight-faced (solemn-faced)
faulds—folds   eatin-airns—fork and knife   lug-held—held to the ear
rinnan—running   owre—over   redds—tidies   aiblins—perhaps
picters—films   sacont hoose—second house
wants his licht—needs his understanding

Daunders out the West Sands 'on the loose'.
Whatever tis,
The waater slorps frae his elbucks as he synds his phiz.

And this is aa the life he kens there is.

daunders—walks easily   slorps—runs off   elbucks—elbows
synds—washes   phiz—face   kens—knows

HAMISH HENDERSON (b. 1919)

From *Elegies for the Dead in Cyrenaica*

First Elegy, End of a Campaign

There are many dead in the brutish desert,
                who lie uneasy
among the scrub in this landscape of half-wit
stunted ill-will. For the dead land is insatiate
and necrophilous. The sand is blowing about still.
Many who for various reasons, or because
                of mere unanswerable compulsion, came here
and fought among the clutching gravestones,
                shivered and sweated,
cried out, suffered thirst, were stoically silent, cursed
the spittering machine-guns, were homesick for Europe
and fast embedded in quicksand of Africa
                agonized and died.
And sleep now. Sleep here the sleep of the dust.

There were our own, there were the others.
Their deaths were like their lives, human and animal.
There were no gods and precious few heroes.
What they regretted when they died had nothing to do with
            ˙ race and leader, realm indivisible,
laboured Augustan speeches or vague imperial heritage.
(They saw through that guff before the axe fell.)
                Their longing turned to
the lost world glimpsed in the memory of letters:

an evening at the pictures in the friendly dark,
two knowing conspirators smiling and whispering secrets;
    or else
a family gathering in the homely kitchen
with Mum so proud of her boys in uniform:
                their thoughts trembled
between moments of estrangement, and ecstatic moments
of reconciliation: and their desire
crucified itself against the unutterable shadow of someone
whose photo was in their wallets.
Then death made his incision.

There were our own, there were the others.
Therefore, minding the great word of Glencoe's
son, that we should not disfigure ourselves
with villainy of hatred; and seeing that all
have gone down like curs into anonymous silence,
I will bear witness for I knew the others.
Seeing that littoral and interior are alike indifferent
and the birds are drawn again to our welcoming north
why should I not sing *them*, the dead, the innocent?

Third Elegy, Leaving the City

Morning After. Get moving. Cheerio. Be seeing you
when this party's over. Right, driver, get weaving.

The truck pulls out
along the corniche. We dismiss with the terseness
of a newsreel the casino and the column,
the scrofulous sellers of obscenity,
the garries, the girls and the preposterous skyline.

Leave them. And out past the stinking tanneries,
the maritime Greek cafes, the wogs and the nets
drying among seaweed. Through the periphery of the city
itching under flagrant sunshine. Faster. We are nearing
the stretch leading to the salt-lake Mareotis.
Sand now, and dust-choked fig-trees. This is the road
where convoys are ordered to act in case of ambush.
A straight run through now to the coastal sector.

One sudden thought wounds: it's a half-hour or over
since we saw the last skirt. And for a moment we regret
the women, and the harbour with a curve so perfect
it seems it was drawn with the mouseion's protractor.

Past red-rimmed eye of the salt-lake. So long then,
holy filth of the living. We are going to the familiar
filth of your negation, to rejoin the proletariat
of levelling death. Stripes are shed and ranks levelled
in death's proletariat. There the Colonel of Hussars,
the keen Sapper Subaltern with a first in economics
and the sergeant well known in international football
crouch with Jock and Jame in their holes like helots.
Distinctions become vain, and former privileges quite
    pointless
in that new situation. See our own and the opponents
advance, meet and merge: the commingled columns
lock, strain, disengage and join issue with the dust.

Do not regret
that we have still in history to suffer
or comrade that we are the agents
of a dialectic that can destroy us
but like a man prepared, like a brave man
bid farewell to the city, and quickly
move forward on the road leading west by the salt-lake.
Like a man for long prepared, like a brave man,
like to the man who was worthy of such a city
be glad that the case admits no other solution,
acknowledge with pride the clear imperative of action
and bid farewell to her, to Alexandria, whom you are losing.

And these, advancing from the direction of Sollum,
swaddies in tropical kit, lifted in familiar vehicles
are they mirage—ourselves out of a mirror?
No, they too, leaving the plateau of Marmarica
for the serpentine of the pass, they advancing towards us
along the coast road, are the others, the brothers
in death's proletariat, they are our victims and betrayers
advancing by the sea-shore to the same assignation.
We send them our greetings out of the mirror.

ALEXANDER SCOTT (b. 1920)

Haar in Princes Street

The heicht o the biggins is happit in rauchens o haar,
　　　The statues alane
　　Stand clearly, heid til fit in stane,
And lour frae *then* and *thonder* at *hencefurth* and *here*.

The past on pedestals, girnan frae ilka feature,
　　　Wi granite frouns
　　They glower at the present's feckless loons,
Its gangrels tint i the haar that fankles the future.

The fowk o flesh, stravaigan wha kens whither,
　　　And come frae whar,
　　Hudder like ghaists i the gastrous haar,
Forfochten and wae i the smochteran smore o the weather.

They swaiver and flirn i the freeth like straes i the sea,
　　　An airtless swither,
　　Steeran awa the t'ane frae t'ither,
Alane, and lawlie aye to be lanesome sae.

But heich i the lift (whar the haar is skailan fairlie
　　　In blufferts o wind)
　　And blacker nor nicht whan starns are blind,
The Castle looms, a fell, a fabulous ferlie.

heicht—height　　haar—mist　　biggins—buildings　　happit—covered
rauchens—mantles　　heid til fit—head to foot　　thonder—yonder
girnan—grimacing　　ilka—every　　frouns—frowns　　feckless—incapable
loons—boys　　gangrels—tramps, wanderers　　tint—lost
fankles—entangles　　fowk—folk　　stravaigan—wandering　　whar—where
hudder—huddle　　ghaists—ghosts　　gastrous—monstrous
forfochten—tired out　　wae—sad　　smochteran—smothering
smore—suffocation　　swaiver—totter　　flirn—twist　　freeth—foam
straes—straws　　airtless—without direction
t'ane frae t'ither—the one from the other　　lawlie—loath
lanesome—lonely　　sae—so　　lift—sky　　skailan—dispersing
fairlie—in good measure　　blufferts—gusts　　nicht—night　　starns—stars
fell—terrible　　ferlie—wonder

Dragonish, darksome, dourlie grapplan the Rock
Wi claws o stane
That scart our historie bare til the bane,
It braks like Fate throu Time's wanchancy reek.

dourlie—stubbornly   scart—scratch   bane—bone   braks—breaks
wanchancy—evil boding   reek—smoke

Continent o Venus

She lies ablow my body's lust and love,
A country dearly-kent, and yet sae fremd
That she's at aince thon Tir-nan-Og I've dreamed,
The airt I've lived in, whar I mean to live,
And mair, much mair, a mixter-maxter warld
Whar fact and dream are taigled up and snorled.

I ken ilk bay o aa her body's strand,
Yet ken them new ilk time I come to shore,
For she's the uncharted sea whar I maun fare
To find anither undiscovered land,
To find it fremd, and yet to find it dear,
To seek for't aye, and aye be bydan there.

dearly-kent—dearly-known   fremd—strange   Tir-nan-Og—land of youth
airt—place   mair—more   mixter-maxter—mixed up   taigled—entangled
snorled—knotted   ken—know   maun—must   bydan—staying

Sang Sonnet

Sing frae the hert, but set the harns til rhyme,
For thochtless words, thae banes that want the marraw,
Maun brak like kindlin ablow the aix o time,
And glaikit sangs can cowp the aipple-barraw,
Dingan the aipples doun in fousome stour
To dee forgotten, tint in thon same hour.

harns—brains   want—lack   kindlin—splinters (wood for kindling)
aix—axe   glaikit—silly   cowp—overturn   dingan—cast down
fousome—dirty   stour—dust   dee—die   tint—lost

A makar scrieved a hunder year sinsyne
Sae mony beuks the press ran short o letters,
But nou there's fient the sowl could say a line
O' aa the lines he whummled out (puir craiturs),
Like brander-muck they're soopit doun the drain
Afore the flood o time, the skaichan rain.

Anither scrievit only ae bit sang,
Sae skeelie-short that time can wark nae wrang.

makar—poet   scrieved—wrote   sinsyne—ago   beuks—books
fient—not one   whummled—tossed   brander—sewer-grid   soopit—swept
skaichan rain—rain that scavenges   skeelie—skilful

Birds in Winter

Winter the warld, albeid the winnock pane
    Has flouers o frost as bricht as spring's.
The cloods the sea-maws scour are kirkyaird stane,
Gray and cauld and lourd on skaichan wings.

The peerie birds in ilka naukit tree,
    Quaet they sit as cones o fir.
Langsyne they skimmed the lift, stravaigan free,
But grippit in winter's neive they canna stir.

They canna stir. The sea-maws up and doun
    Gang ower and ower and ower the sky.
The peeries wait for death wi niver a soun,
The sea-maws rax for life wi niver a cry.

albeid—although   winnock—window   flouers—flowers   bricht—bright
cloods—clouds   sea-maws—sea-gulls   lourd—heavy   skaichan—scavenging
peerie—small   ilka—every   naukit—naked   quaet—quiet
langsyne—long ago   lift—sky   stravaigan—wandering   neive—fist
canna—cannot   gang—go   ower—over   peeries—small birds
niver—never   rax—stretch

EDWIN MORGAN (b. 1920)

King Billy

Grey over Riddrie the clouds piled up,
dragged their rain through the cemetery trees.
The gates shone cold. Wind rose
flaring the hissing leaves, the branches
swung, heavy, across the lamps.
Gravestones huddled in drizzling shadow,
flickering streetlights scanned the requiescats,
a name and an urn, a date, a dove
picked out, lost, half regained.
What is this dripping wreath, blown from its grave
red, white, blue, and gold
'To Our Leader of Thirty Years Ago'—

Bareheaded, in dark suits, with flutes
and drums, they brought him here, in procession
seriously, King Billy of Brigton, dead,
from Bridgeton Cross: a memory of violence,
brooding days of empty bellies,
billiard smoke and a sour pint,
boots or fists, famous sherrickings,
the word, the scuffle, the flash, the shout,
bloody crumpling in the close,
bricks for papish windows, get
the Conks next time, the Conks ambush
the Billy Boys, the Billy Boys the Conks till
Sillitoe scuffs the razors down the stank—
No, but it isn't the violence they remember
but the legend of a violent man
born poor, gang-leader in the bad times
of idleness and boredom, lost in better days,
a bouncer in a betting club,
a quiet man at last, dying
alone in Bridgeton in a box bed.
So a thousand people stopped the traffic
for the hearse of a folk hero and the flutes
threw 'Onward Christian Soldiers' to the winds

from unironic lips, the mourners kept
in step, and there were some who wept.

Go from the grave. The shrill flutes
are silent, the march dispersed.
Deplore what is to be deplored,
and then find out the rest.

The Death of Marilyn Monroe

What innocence? Whose guilt? What eyes? Whose breast?
Crumpled orphan, nembutal bed,
white hearse, Los Angeles,
DiMaggio! Los Angeles! Miller! Los Angeles!
    America!
That Death should seem the only protector—
That all arms should have faded, and the great cameras
    and lights become an inquisition and a torment—
That the many acquaintances, the autograph-hunters,
    the inflexible directors, the drive-in admirers
    should become a blur of incomprehension and
    pain—
That lonely Uncertainty should limp up, grinning,
    with bewildering barbiturates, and watch her
    undress and lie down and in her anguish
call for him! call for him to strengthen her with what
    could only dissolve her! A method
of dying, we are shaken, we see it. Strasberg!
Los Angeles! Olivier! Los Angeles! Others die
and yet by this death we are a little shaken, we feel it,
America.
Let no one say communication is a cantword.
They had to lift her hand from the bedside telephone.
But what she had not been able to say
perhaps she had said. 'All I had was my life.
I have no regrets, because if I made
any mistakes, I was responsible.
There is now—and there is the future.
What has happened is behind. So
it follows you around? So what?'—This
to a friend, ten days before.

And so she was responsible.
And if she was not responsible, not wholly responsible,
    Los Angeles? Los Angeles? Will it follow you
    around? Will the slow white hearse of the child
    of America follow you around?

DERICK THOMSON (b. 1921)

Nuair a Thill mi gu T'uaigh

Nuair a thill mi gu t'uaigh
gu tairiseach, tlàth
cha bu chuimhne leam t'fhiamh.

Bha ceò air mo shùil;
dh'fhalbh seachd is seachd bliadhna
le craiceann nan làmh
a dh'aithnicheadh do chneas;
bhuail na tuinn air mo chlaistneachd;
bha m'iarrtas is m'ùidh
bàthte fo shùgh liath-uaine, fo chlàr
sgìth mo bheatha.

Rinn fàileadh nan Sìthean tais a' chiad bheàrn
air an sgàile sin 's i seachd-fillte.

Troimh fhilleadh na Sàbaid
chuimhnich mi air do chràbhadh;
troimh fhilleadh Luain
dh'fhairich mi tarraing a' chuain;
troimh fhilleadh Mhàirt
dh' éirich do chruadal an àird;
troimh fhilleadh Chiadain
chunnaic mi thu air chiallaidh;
am filleadh Dhir-daoin
bha do bhanais 's do mhaoin;
fo fhilleadh na h-Aoine
bha 'phìob is na h-òrain fhaoine;

110

troimh fhilleadh na Sathuirn
dh' aithnich mi nach biodh rath oirnn.

Is bha thu agam—
brèagh, bòidheach, beothant,
milis, mòdhar,
cho diombuain ri flùr,
O shaoghail a bh' ann.

When, Tender and Mild
(Translation by Iain Crichton Smith)

When, tender and mild,
I came to your grave,
I could not remember
your frown or your smile.

There were tears in my eyes:
for seven and seven years
had taken the skin
from the hand that once knew
the skin of your flesh.
Waves beat in my ears:
my love and desire
were buried beneath
the grey green ooze
the Minch of my life.

The scent of the flowers
made the first light
in that seven-fold shade.

Through the fold of the Sunday
I knew your devotion;
through the fold of the Monday
the ocean was calling;
through the fold of the Tuesday
your courage arose;
through the fold of the Wednesday
I saw you at fasting;
through the fold of the Thursday
was your gear and your marriage;

through the fold of the Friday
was the piping and singing;
in Saturday's fold
our ill-luck was told.

And I held you, then—
lively and lovely,
sweetly and gently—
O transient flower,
O world that is gone.

Cruaidh?

Cuil-lodair, is Briseadh na h-Eaglaise,
is briseadh nan tacannan—
lamhachas-làidir dà thrian de ar comas;
'se seòltachd tha dhìth oirnn.
Nuair a theirgeas a' chruaidh air faobhar na speala
caith bhuat a' chlach-lìomhaidh;
chan eil agad ach iarunn bog
mur eil de chruas 'nad innleachd na ni sgathadh.

Is caith bhuat briathran mìne
oir chan fhada bhios briathran agad;
tha Tuatha Dé Danann fo'n talamh,
tha Tìr nan Og anns an Fhraing,
's nuair a ruigeas tu Tìr a' Gheallaidh,
mura bi thu air t' aire,
coinnichidh Sasunnach riut is plìon air,
a dh'innse dhut gun tug Dia, bràthair athar, còir dha
     as an fhearann.

Steel?

Culloden, the Disruption,
and the breaking up of the tack-farms—
two thirds of our power is violence;
it is cunning we need.

When the tempered steel near the edge of the
    scythe-blade is worn,
throw away the whetstone;
you have nothing left but soft iron
unless your intellect has a steel edge that will cut clean.

And throw away soft words,
for soon you will have no words left;
the Tuatha De Danann[1] are underground,
the Land of the Ever-Young is in France,
and when you reach the Promised Land,
unless you are on your toes,
a bland Englishman will meet you,
and say to you that God, his uncle, has given him a
    title to the land.

GEORGE MACKAY BROWN (b. 1921)

Our Lady of the Waves

The twenty brothers of Eynhallow
Have made a figure of Our Lady.
From red stone they carved her
And set her on a headland.
There spindrift salts her feet.
At dawn the brothers sang this
        Blessed Lady, since midnight
        We have done three things.
        We have bent hooks.
        We have patched a sail.
        We have sharpened knives.
        Yet the little silver brothers are afraid.
        Bid them come to our net.
        Show them our fire, our fine round plates.
        Per Dominum Christum nostrum
        Look mildly on our hungers.

[1] *Tuatha De Danann*, a supernatural race in Ireland, sometimes said to be the progenitors of the fairies.

The codling hang in a row by the wall.
At noon the brothers sang this
    Holy Mother, Una the cow
    Gives thin blue milk.
    Where is the golden thread of butter?
    The stone in the middle of our glebe
    Has deep black roots.
    We have broken three ploughs on it.
    Per Christum Dominum nostrum
    Save Una from the axe,
    Our dappled cow with large eyes.

The girls go by with pails to the byre.
At sunset the brothers sang this
    Sweet Virgin, the woman of Garth
    Is forever winking at Brother Paul.
    She puts an egg in his palm.
    She lays peats in his cowl.
    Her neck is long as spilt milk.
    Brother Paul is a good lad.
    Well he carries word and wine for the priest.
    But three red midnights
    His tongue has run loose among dreams.

Paul has broken knees at the stone.
At midnight the brothers sang this
    Queen of Heaven, this good day
    There is a new cradle at Quoys.
    It rocks on the blue floor.
    And there is a new coffin at Hamnavoe.
    Arnor the poet lies there
    Tired of words and wounds.
    In between, what is man?
    A head bent over fish and bread and ale.
    Outside, the long furrow.
    Through a door, a board with a shape on it.

    Guard the plough and the nets.
    Star of the sea, shine for us.

Hamnavoe Market

They drove to the Market with ringing pockets.

Folster found a girl
Who put wounds on his face and throat,
Small and diagonal, like red doves.

Johnston stood beside the barrel.
All day he stood there.
He woke in a ditch, his mouth full of ashes.

Grieve bought a balloon and a goldfish.
He swung through the air.
He fired shotguns, rolled pennies, ate sweet fog from a stick.

Heddle was at the Market also.
I know nothing of his activities.
He is and always was a quiet man.

Garson fought three rounds with a negro boxer,
And received thirty shillings,
Much applause, and an eye loaded with thunder.

Where did they find Flett?
They found him in a brazen circle,
All flame and blood, a new Salvationist.

A gypsy saw in the hand of Halcro
Great strolling herds, harvests, a proud woman.
He wintered in the poorhouse.

They drove home from the Market under the stars
Except for Johnston
Who lay in a ditch, his mouth full of dying fires.

The Finished House

In the finished house, a flame is brought to the hearth.
Then a table, between door and window
Where a stranger will eat before the men of the house.
A bed is laid in a secret corner
For the three agonies—love, birth, death—
That are made beautiful with ceremony.
The neighbours come with gifts—
A set of cups, a calendar, some chairs,
A fiddle is hung at the wall.
A girl puts lucky salt in a dish.
The cupboard has its loaf and bottle.
On the seventh morning
One spills water of blessing over the threshold.

Wedding

With a great working of elbows
The fiddlers ranted
      —Joy to Ingrid and Magnus!

With much boasting and burning
The whisky circled
      —Wealth to Ingrid and Magnus!

With deep clearings of the throat
The minister intoned
      —Thirdly, Ingrid and Magnus. . .

Ingrid and Magnus stared together
When midnight struck
At a white unbroken bed.

116

Willag

As one would say, lighting an evening pipe
In the village street
'Tatties will soon be ripe
And sweet in the mouth this year
Having been planted dry,'
So Willag, before the boat turned over
Shouted to them on the shore,
'Drive my cow and sheep from the oats
Into the wild white clover,
And Brech can have my horse for his five goats'.

Then his boots filled, and Willag said no more.

Saint Magnus in Birsay

What did they bring for the day of the saint?
The shepherd a fleece.
That winter many lambs were born in the snow.

What did the ditch people take?
The tinkers brought
A new bright can. Their hammers beat all night.

What did the sea give to Magnus?
Seven young fishermen
Laid a torn net at the wall of the church.

And the farm boys offered
A gaiety, sweetness, chastity
Of hymning mouths.

The women came to their martyr
With woven things
And salt butter from the poor of the islands.

And the poor of the islands
Brought their hungers.
They went home with crossed hands over the hill.

IAN HAMILTON FINLAY (b. 1925)

Black Tomintoul

To Scotland came the tall American
And went to stay on a little farm
Oh it was a Scotch farm set in the wild
A wee Scotch burn and a stoney field

She came to a corner, it was raining
And the little trees were all leaning in
This was Scotland the way she had thought of it
Care, not gravity, makes them lean
The rain falling Scotchly, Scotchly
And the hills that did not soar up but in

But most she looked at the bull so wild
She looked at the bull with the eyes of a child
Never in New York did she see such a bull
As this great Scotch one, Tomintoul
She called him secretly, the great Scotch bull.

He was black all over, even for a bull
And oh he had such a lovely hide
She saw him follow one cow aside
Tell me, please, is that cow his bride?

No, they are all his lawful br-r-ride
There were twentyfour cows on the Scotch hillside

It was almost too much for the tall American girl
She watched him stand on his opposite hill
Black Tomintoul, and he always bellowed
But afterwards something in her was mellowed.

ALASTAIR REID (b. 1926)

Growing, Flying, Happening

Say the soft bird's name, but do not be surprised
to see it fall
headlong, struck skyless, into its pigeonhole—
columba palambus and you have it dead,
wedged, neat, unwinged in your head.

That the black-backed tatter-winged thing
straking the harbour water and then plummeting
down, to come up, sleek head-a-cock,
a minted herring shining in its beak,
is a guillemot, is neither here nor there
in the amazement of its rising,
wings slicing the stiff salt air.

That of the spindling spear-leaved plant,
wearing the palest purple umbel,
many-headed, blue-tinted, stilt-stalked
at the stream-edge, one should say briefly
angelica, is not enough (though grant
the name itself to be beautiful).
Grant too that any name
makes its own music: that *bryony, sally-my-handsome,*
burst at their sound into flower,
and that *falcon* and *phalarope* fly off in the ear,
still,
names are for saying at home.

the point is seeing—the grace
beyond recognition, the ways
of the bird rising, unnamed, unknown,
beyond the range of language, beyond its noun.
Eyes open on growing, flying, happening,
and go on opening. Manifold, the world
dawns on unrecognising, realising eyes.
Amazement is the thing.
Not love, but the astonishment of loving.

IAIN CRICHTON SMITH (b. 1928)

Old Woman

And she, being old, fed from a mashed plate
as an old mare might droop across a fence
to the dull pastures of its ignorance.
Her husband held her upright while he prayed

to God who is all-forgiving to send down
some angel somewhere who might land perhaps
in his foreign wings among the gradual crops.
She munched, half dead, blindly searching the spoon.

Outside, the grass was raging. There I sat
imprisoned in my pity and my shame
that men and women having suffered time
should sit in such a place, in such a state

and wished to be away, yes, to be far away
with athletes, heroes, Greeks or Roman men
who pushed their bitter spears into a vein
and would not spend an hour with such decay.

'Pray God,' he said, 'we ask you, God,' he said.
The bowed back was quiet. I saw the teeth
tighten their grip around a delicate death.
And nothing moved within the knotted head

but only a few poor veins as one might see
vague wishless seaweed floating on a tide
of all the salty waters where had died
too many waves to mark two more or three.

Luss Village

Such walls, like honey, and the old are happy
in morphean air like gold-fish in a bowl.
Ripe roses trail their margins down a sleepy
mediaeval treatise on the slumbering soul.

And even the water, fabulously silent,
has no salt tales to tell us, nor makes jokes
about the yokel mountains, huge and patient,
that will not court her but read shadowy books.

A world so long departed! In the churchyard
the tilted tombs still gossip, and the leaves
of stony testaments are read by Richard,
Jean and Carol, pert among the sheaves

of unscythed shadows, while the noon day hums
with bees and water and the ghosts of psalms.

A Note on Puritans

There was no curtain between them and fire.
Every moment was a moment when
a man could sink into a tranced despair
or shake his heels to vanity and turn
with frenzied gaiety from that drying air.

Therefore their urgency. That fire glowed
along their darkened senses, hour by hour.
Only the book they clutched so tightly cheered
hearts that might stop, eyes that their burning fear
could hole with flame: heads that their thoughts had charred.

Garden and gardener, book and reader glowed:
limbs crackled their sins: silks twitched in a blue flame:
a man's flesh melted in the mouth of God:
he lost his name to earn a lasting name.
A heaven flashed where all that oil flowed.

That was great courage to have watched that fire,
not placing a screen before it as we do
with pictures, poems, landscapes, a great choir
of mounting voices which can drown the raw
hissing and spitting of flame with other fire.

That was great courage to have stayed as true
to truth as man can stay. From them we learn
how certain truths can make men brutish too:
how few can watch the bared teeth slow-burn
and not be touched by the lumps of fire they chew

into contempt and barrenness. I accuse
these men of singleness and loss of grace
who stared so deeply into the fire's hues
that all was fire to them.

                        Yes, to this place
they should return. Cheeks have the fire men choose.

Schoolgirl on Speech-day in the Open Air

Here in their health and youth they're sitting down
on thick tight grass while bald official men,
heavy with sunshine, wear a moment's crown
and put it by reluctantly again.

I look at one who lies upon her side,
wearing bright yellow for the clasping light.
No ring of shadow has engaged her pride
or wolfed her, fallen, in the circling night.

Her scorn springs out like swords. A smile plays round
her unstained lips, as if a joke would spill.
She turns her shining head into that sound
which stumbles downward from low hill to hill.

And then I turn again and see how one
dangles her will from every word he spins
and think how thirty years can fence a man
by what he loses and by what he wins

122

into a little ground where he can see
the golden landlords, pursed with luck, stride past.
And schoolgirls flashing by are far and free
as fish he played for but new men will taste.

And the timed applause which falls from rock to rock
and then to silence is the way he came.
She gathers, like necessity, her cloak.
The schoolgirl rises—and must do the same.

Two Girls Singing

It neither was the words nor yet the tune.
Any tune would have done and any words.
Any listener or no listener at all.

As nightingales in rocks or a child crooning
in its own world of strange awakening
or larks for no reason but themselves.

So on the bus through late November running
by yellow lights tormented, darkness falling,
the two girls sang for miles and miles together

and it wasn't the words or tune. It was the singing.
It was the human sweetness in that yellow,
the unpredicted voices of our kind.

Old Highland Lady Reading Newspaper

Grasping the newspaper in kneaded hands
in her ordered bed, the tablets at the side,
she slowly reads of all her friends who've died
in the black holds of the approaching islands

where the horses and the daffodils are dead,
unfashionable skirts have swirled away
down the Dutch cornfields and the fields of hay
into the numerous caves of her bald head

bent over print and old remorseless hands
grasping these deaths, the tombstones all in white
her eyes traverse with gritty appetite
in the slow justice of her mouth's small sounds.

Johnson in the Highlands

A reasoning mind travels through this country.
In these sad wastes a Londoner by choice
sees water falling, and some meagre deer.

Examines with his tough reasoning mind
lochs, deer, and people: is not seduced
by Mrs. Radcliffe's green hysteria

from a musical prose we've never once achieved,
whose fences cannot reach between the words
whose arguments are broken-backed with exile.

A classical sanity considers Skye.
A huge hard light falls across shifting hills.
This mind, contemptuous of miracles

and beggarly sentiment, illuminates
a healthy moderation. But I hear
like a native dog notes beyond his range

the modulations of a queer music
twisting his huge black body in the pain
that shook him also in raw blazing London.

STEWART CONN (b. 1936)

Todd

My father's white uncle became
Arthritic and testamental in
Lyrical stages. He held cardinal sin
Was misuse of horses, then any game

Won on the sabbath. A Clydesdale
To him was not bells and sugar or declension
From paddock, but primal extension
Of rock and soil. Thundered nail

Turned to sacred bolt. And each night
In the stable he would slaver and slave
At cracked hooves, or else save
Bowls of porridge for just the right

Beast. I remember I lied
To him once, about oats: then I felt
The brand of his loving tongue, the belt
Of his own horsey breath. But he died,

When the mechanised tractor came to pass.
Now I think of him neighing to some saint
In a simple heaven or, beyond complaint,
Leaning across a fence and munching grass.

Simon

He is no dankness in the mind
Of a child nor, huddling, builds
Dark memories. His simple kind
Is not finally coffined in fields

Of clay but boxed, sunlit, on grass.
He trembled; his flint-scrubbed
Fingers did pruning; his mass
Was neat flower-beds where, robed

In lilac, he fumbled. He picked
Polished apples, then weeded
The plainsong path. Cats licked
His wrists; fierce dogs tried

To nuzzle. They wanted to put him away
When he started smiling at bird
And human alike, with delicacy.
But he withered and went of his own accord.

ROBIN FULTON (b. 1937)

Meeting in Early Winter

Autumn has been swept from the fields, battened down
In stacks, pulled tight against winter.
The man, whose small eyes noticed each
Stone on the once more sterile slope,
Was content that another year's work was done.

At the gate a moving shadow became his priest
(A figure at births, deaths and marriages
But he only sometimes understood the land):
The shadow passed curtly and shrank. They agreed
About the long nights and the rough sea at least.

Alone again, forgetting the quick soft
Priestly words, he stopped and for a second
Saw exactly: waves ambush a rock,
Black hills lean downwards, and his own
Kitchen light blinking from the croft.

STIRLING COUNTY LIBRARY

Index of First Lines